Hard Labour

wage theft in the age of inequality

Ben Schneiders

SCRIBE

Melbourne • London

Scribe Publications
18-20 Edward St, Brunswick, Victoria 3056, Australia
2 John St, Clerkenwell, London, WC1N 2ES, United Kingdom
3754 Pleasant Ave, Suite 100, Minneapolis, Minnesota 55409, USA

Published by Scribe 2022

Typeset in Adobe Caslon Pro by the publishers

Printed and bound in Australia by Griffin Press

Scribe is committed to the sustainable use of natural resources and the use of paper products made responsibly from those resources.

Scribe acknowledges Australia's First Nations peoples as the traditional owners and custodians of this country. We recognise that sovereignty was never ceded, and we pay our respects to their elders, past and present.

978 1 922585 32 5 (Australian edition)
978 1 922586 67 4 (ebook)

A catalogue record for this book is available from the
National Library of Australia.

scribepublications.com.au
scribepublications.co.uk
scribepublications.com

To Sarah, Sebastian, Isaac, Harriet, and for those to come.

Glossary of trade unions

Australian Council of Trade Unions (ACTU)
Australian Education Union (AEU)
Australian Manufacturing Workers' Union (AMWU)
Australian Nursing and Midwifery Federation (ANMF)
Australian Workers' Union (AWU)
Construction, Forestry, Maritime, Mining & Energy Union
(CFMMEU)
National Tertiary Education Union (NTEU)
National Union of Workers (NUW)
Retail and Fast Food Workers Union (RAFFWU)
Shop, Distributive and Allied Employees' Association (SDA)
Transport Workers' Union (TWU)
United Workers Union (UWU)

Contents

Introduction

The symptoms of rising inequality are visible all around us—especially in the celebration of excess and extreme wealth, and the vastly different worlds people inhabit while living in the same country or even a few suburbs away in the same city. Even how likely someone was to get sick and die of Covid-19 in the first few years of the pandemic was shaped by these material divides. Whether it is over access to private education, private health, private housing, adequate superannuation, or the jobs that people get to do, a whirring, self-perpetuating inequality machine has been created in Australia. It runs from the cradle to the grave, creating a parallel society for those who have the good fortune to access the gilded system or are born into it. The machine now appears nearly impossible to stop or slow. Rising inequality, along with climate change, are the major crises of our age, undermining democracy.

Some Australians have lives of great privilege, unparalleled in human history. Less often acknowledged is another side to this prosperity. About one-quarter to one-third of the workforce is locked in a cycle of precarity through job insecurity, low pay, and, often, wage theft. A large, sprawling de facto guest-worker program of up to one million non-citizens on a range of work and student visas has been created, mostly servicing the wealthy, and the affluent middle class. Most of these facts are obscured from view, not part of the dominant narrative of what Australians tell themselves about life in this country. Yet these experiences are real and are a fundamental challenge to Australia's political and economic system, which was built through the twentieth century, and produced far greater levels of material equality. Based on statistical measures of income inequality (see Graphs One and Two), Australia has not been this consistently unequal since the 1930s, and is now more unequal than many of the countries in the OECD, ranking thirteenth out of thirty-eight countries. It is more unequal, by income, than Poland, Greece, and Ireland. When we measure inequality by wealth, the gap is still wider. It is a great time to be rich.

When we look to the US, or parts of Europe, we can also see the effects of growing inequality: the lack of hope for a better future, and the lure of the authoritarian leader. Whether the same forces could formalise and take root here is debated, but if we look closely we can see their presence, albeit not yet in such sharp relief. There is the collapse of trust in our system to deliver opportunity as extensively as before, and a gravitation away from major parties to the often unhinged and to the conspiracy theorists. There is the spectacle of the billionaire Clive Palmer tapping into anti-vaccination sentiment to become a voice for those opposed to the status quo, even though there are few greater beneficiaries from it than him. It is a now-familiar dynamic that led to Donald Trump becoming a US president. At its heart is often a sense of powerlessness and a distrust that the institutions that have shaped Western democracies still work, or ever did. Or that there are credible pathways to a better life.

Australia has become seriously rich since the 1980s, as we opened our economy more fully to global capital and trade flows, and as China boomed. We can see the exaltation of great wealth, the tens of billions owned by Twiggy Forrest, Mike Cannon-Brookes, or Gina Rinehart. These were unimaginable sums a few decades ago. The richest Australian in 2001 was Kerry Packer, worth $6.2 billion. Twenty years later, the richest Australian was mining heir Gina Rinehart, who was worth $31 billion, her wealth having tripled in a decade. Yet the rising tide has not lifted all boats. Many have been left behind, particularly those with low levels of education. Once, people without assets could make a good life for themselves. Now, less so. Those without degrees earn about 50 per cent less than those with a higher education. An analysis of Bureau of Statistics data shows those with less education report having poor or fair health at twice the level of the most educated. All this breeds resentment, as people often feel intuitively that the system is stacked against them.

And a more unequal society manifests itself in all sorts of ways — some obvious, some less so. It can be observed in the different choices people have to make, whether it is to work outside the home in Covid-exposed sectors and risk illness, to have the burden of high debt and job insecurity, to never own a home, or to retire with few savings. All of this is shaped by the lottery of birth, class, gender, race, and the suburb or town that you were born into. Inequality matters. It condemns many of us to unnecessarily harder lives, and it is fundamentally undemocratic, based often on inheritance and who gets access to the best education, the best healthcare and jobs, and the opportunities to more fully develop their talents. Yet inequality, much like climate change, may increase too slowly to create a vivid and immediate existential crisis in the way the pandemic has. Eventually, much like climate change, rising inequality causes fundamental changes to a society, as we have seen in countries with the sharpest disparities of wealth and income. It is the path to social upheaval and authoritarianism, to social revolutions, and to growing distrust and contempt. Much like climate change, when left to run wild, it becomes much harder to fix.

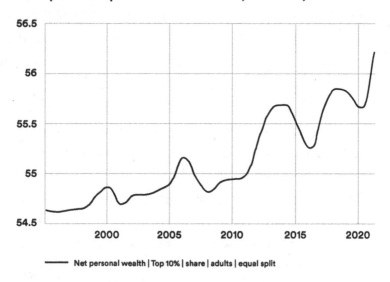

Top 10% net personal wealth share, Australia, 1995–2021

Net personal wealth | Top 10% | share | adults | equal split

GRAPH ONE *Source: World Inequality Database*

The pandemic has proved to be no leveller either. While we were told we were 'all in this together', the wealth of the richest few hundred Australians surged. The worst effects of the pandemic were felt by those in insecure work in the most disadvantaged suburbs of Melbourne and Sydney, either through catching the virus itself or losing work. Tens of thousands of temporary migrants were denied access to government support. Long queues were seen outside charities and food banks. Having a large temporary-worker program meant that all the costs and risks were borne by these workers. In April 2020, senior federal government ministers told them that if they could not support themselves, it was time for them to go home as quickly as possible — a brutal message to people who had contributed so much to the country as students and workers.

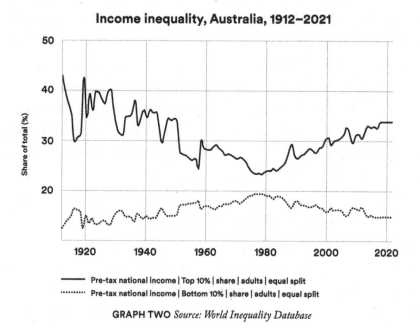

Income inequality, Australia, 1912–2021

GRAPH TWO *Source: World Inequality Database*

There was little pushback, or ability to push back. These were non-citizens, and few were union members. There were next to no jobs for these guest workers, with their workplaces in areas such as hospitality often shut due to lockdowns and the pandemic. Capital is now so powerful, and the system so stacked against workers and unions, that the people the unions most urgently need to represent aren't even citizens anymore.

More than a century ago, in the early years of the twentieth century, the labour movement transformed the country, no matter how unevenly, for the better. It used strikes and the collective power of workers to create an Australia partially in its own image. Most famously, in the *Harvester* decision of 1907, the courts mandated a version of a living wage to workers. That decision set the tone for decades. The gains for working people were real. Labor governments were formed, and life for many was much better than in other parts of the rich world—where, at that time in the US, for example, workers on strike or campaigning for better pay and conditions were still being killed by bosses and their proxies into the 1920s. Here, representatives of workers helped form governments.

For half of the twentieth century, a social bargain held in Australia. The labour movement remained strong, wages high, and the economy mostly closed through the imposition of protectionist trade policies, although the fundamental conflicts between labour and capital remained. There were many downsides to prosperity, and this narrow version of the 'working man's paradise' was founded on unstable and discriminatory grounds. The abundance of cheap land and resources, a source of much wealth, was stolen from Indigenous Australians. Migrant labour from Asia was kept out through racist laws. Women propped up this system through unpaid and under-recognised domestic labour. By the 1970s, the system was stalling both here and overseas. Legalised racism was becoming untenable as the oppressed and colonised challenged it. Separately, both here and in other parts of the rich world, the collapse of the Keynesian model led to new pressures. Amid high unemployment and inflation, the profitability of business and returns on capital had become too uneven as union strength claimed a bigger share of national income for workers. Business leaders were in revolt and wanted change to the post-war order, which had been shaped by public investment and reconstruction, and, later on, rising union militancy.

From the 1980s onwards, Australia took a new path to boost the returns on capital, to make the economy and system more competitive (see Graph Three). This was sold as a new era of prosperity for all. It was the neo-liberal world that Australia joined and has been living in ever since. Deregulation, privatisation, and free trade were first implemented at scale here by a Labor government. There was a social bargain agreed with the introduction of Medicare, the widespread extension of superannuation, and the retention of an award safety net. All this made for a less harsh adjustment than occurred in Britain, New Zealand, and the US, although real wages still fell in its aftermath and inequality rose. Over time it has transformed the country, unleashing significant wealth but also rising inequality, as the union movement has collapsed under the weight of the demise of manufacturing, the introduction of anti-union laws, and, in part, some of its own failings. Unions went from representing about half the workforce to around 14 per cent. Now, much of the labour movement appears exhausted after decades of decline and attacks. There is little optimism or energy within it.

The public language and norms of the country have changed as it has become more unequal. From the 1980s onwards, former prime minister John Howard was an enthusiastic supporter of privatisation, deregulation, and breaking unions, all the things that contributed to worsening inequality. But he also understood the mood of the country. Howard used the word 'egalitarian' more than 100 times during his time as prime minister, from 1996 to 2007, in speeches and interviews. His contemporary conservative successor, Scott Morrison, never used it while prime minister. 'Aspiration', an Australia of property owners and shareholders, was the theme throughout the Howard and Morrison years, but the language of a more equal Australia has not persisted. There is no longer the need to pretend in the same way.

In many of our imaginations, the working class toil in factories or in high-vis outfits on construction sites. It's an almost entirely male picture. And while these jobs still matter and exist, it is not the 1980s anymore. Industries exposed to trade and competition from China and elsewhere, such as manufacturing, have shrunk in relative numbers, while service and social-assistance jobs, often dominated by women, are now occupied by much of what we could now call the working class. Wages and conditions for many of them are stagnating. In 2010, when the Fair Work laws were introduced, about 1.3 million workers had their pay set by the minimum wage of the award. By 2021, that had grown to 2.7 million. These workers have little ability to lift their wages due to low union density, the proliferation of small firms, and the use of part-time casual roles, as families juggle limited paid work with unpaid caring roles. Without being able to bargain directly with their employer, they are stuck on a minimum-wage cycle.

Net national wealth to net national income ratio, Australia, 1960–2020

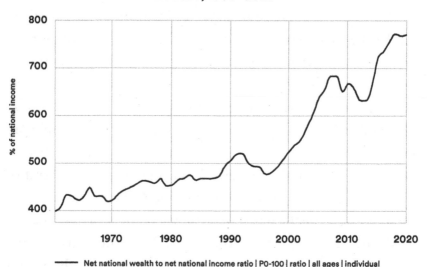

Net national wealth to net national income ratio | P0-100 | ratio | all ages | individual

GRAPH THREE *Source: World Inequality Database*

This book tells the stories of many of the hundreds of workers that I have spoken with, ranging from undocumented workers to those on temporary visas, and to underpaid local workers. All have trusted me with the stories of their experiences and their hopes for a better future. I'll be forever grateful to them, and I hope here to do some justice to what they've said and to make sense of the changes wrought by rising inequality. I've relied heavily on the work of French economist Thomas Piketty for my understanding of that inequality. He has described, so crucially, the growing imbalances between the growth of the economy and the higher returns from capital, which, over time, as he puts it, have had 'powerful and destabilising effects on the structure and dynamics of social inequality'. This book is not, however, a work of economic or political theory. Rather, it seeks to provide some of the finer-grained detail of how inequality has increased, and how power relations have evolved between those with and those without wealth and power.

Since 2015, in my role as an investigative reporter at *The Age*, I've written hundreds of articles about wage theft, mostly with my colleague Royce Millar. The investigative work has exposed more than two dozen companies for underpaying their workers, including some of Australia's largest employers such as Coles, Woolworths, McDonald's, and Chemist Warehouse. It has also exposed some of the most famous restaurants in the country and companies operating across the farming sector. The reporting has contributed to change, whether it has been many hundreds of millions of dollars a year in extra pay or repaid wages, in new laws, and in public pressure. Yet so vast is wage theft in Australia that my work—and that of the people who have worked with me, whether workers or union officials—undoubtedly reveals only a fraction of the problem.

Over the years, I've received significant pushback over my wage-theft reporting—far more than I've received from any of my other work, which has ranged from exposing religious abuses to political corruption. There's been significant pressure, both legal and other kinds, put on me to stop my investigations and reports. Regularly, I've been told that wage theft is due to the industrial relations system being too complex, and that the reporting is unfair to business owners. Or that it is just as common for workers to be overpaid as underpaid. (There is no evidence for this.) I've pushed ahead, as wage theft—to me, at least—is offensive to the idea of a fair society, breaching laws and norms about how people should be treated. It is an assault on the idea of equality, which is a fundamental requirement of a well-functioning democracy. Left unsaid in all this pushback is the assumption that those with money and connections almost have a right to steal, unlike those with nothing, who can be jailed for far smaller thefts.

Through telling these stories in this book, I want to show how some of these business models work and why so many people are left unpaid, underpaid, and exploited. And to show how businesses owned by private equity or by rich families operating through tax havens, or traded on the stock exchange, often operate. I hope to help readers understand what has occurred by looking through the prism of power—who has it, and who does not—and especially to show how a lack of power results in many workers being dominated, and in not having control of essential parts of their lives.

Many casual or labour-hire workers only know if they'll have paid work the next day when they receive a text message the night before. How do they plan ahead to do the things that most people crave? To start a family, to have relationships, to see friends, to own a home? For a temporary migrant worker, the fear is that if they speak up, they could lose their job and then their ability to stay in the country. In a society of abundance, this is how we've decided to construct our political economy for those with the least—basing it on chronic insecurity.

This book also tells the story of failed institutions: the industrial relations regulators and system; in some cases, the unions themselves; and the political system. It seeks to describe how those who own substantial capital are seeing their wealth accelerate, and to discuss the long-term effects of this on inequality, politics, and, in the end, people's ability to live fuller lives.

In Western societies, this rising inequality has held true for much of the last 200 years, according to Piketty's research of economic and financial data. The exception, in much of the rich world, was the unusual post-war period, when post-war reconstruction and progressive taxation reversed that trend for several decades. Since then, wealth and inequality have grown dramatically. Australia, not a major subject of Piketty's work, has had a similar experience, with net national wealth doubling, compared to the overall economy, since the 1970s. That wealth is highly concentrated. Households worth more than $10 million have tripled from 2004 to 2018, while those worth less than zero—because their debts exceed their assets—have doubled to 1.4 per cent of households. Now the top 1 per cent in Australia control more wealth than the bottom 60 per cent of households combined, or more than 15 million people.

At the moment, the prospects for turning around a forty-year redistribution of wealth from labour to capital appear unlikely. The shrinking of the labour movement has given business interests unprecedented power and influence. As we know, some of Australia's biggest companies have engaged in wage theft. However, while the outlook appears grim, change is always possible, and there can be a future for a fairer, more democratic system. The solutions are there before us, at first in small steps and then later in bigger ones.

The federal Albanese Labor government was elected in May 2022 with a more modest policy platform than Labor had presented under Bill Shorten in 2019, when the party targeted some of the worst of the housing and share market tax breaks enjoyed by wealthy investors. Yet it is unlikely that the government will be able to avoid dealing with the problem of rising inequality. As it took office, workers were experiencing the largest fall in real wages in decades, and the government will be forced to make tough choices.

It came under intense pressure both just before and after the election for backing a rise in the minimum wage to match inflation—a hardly radical proposal. The Fair Work Commission in June 2022 endorsed the approach, lifting the wages of the lowest paid by 5.2 per cent and millions of other award-reliant workers by at least 4.6 per cent. The latter increases represented a small real wage cut for those workers, and yet, within weeks of that Fair Work decision, business interests and *The Australian Financial Review* were pressuring the government, and campaigning for unions and workers to accept a cap on wage rises—in effect, a deep real-wage cut. This was despite rising wages not being the cause of higher prices throughout the economy.

It showed how hard it is to reduce inequality, and how committed powerful interests were to maintaining the status quo. But it remains the case that if the Albanese government fails to strike a new political and social compact, increases in political extremism, violence, conspiracy theories, and crime are just some of the ways the pathologies of inequality will assert themselves.

New ideas are needed to support new ways of working, to make workplaces more democratic, to find ways to expand and enrich the lives of all of us. Otherwise, we may one day wake up in a country where some may be rich beyond their dreams but too scared to leave their yachts and walled compounds, while many of us will live lives of unnecessary insecurity and precarity. In different ways, we would all be poorer if that were to happen.

Chapter One

All in this together

When the coronavirus pandemic took off in Sydney's south-west in mid-2021, it was as if Covid-19 had been created with malevolent intent. It was able to seek out and target those who had the least—whether it was pay, power, social status, or job security. For weeks before then, the virus had circulated in the wealthiest parts of Australia's most ostentatious city: the bits from where you can see the glorious water of Sydney harbour, or where it's never too far away. The virus had threatened to break out through the richest areas of the city while never quite doing so.

By mid-2021, the city and the country appeared to be on edge, waiting to see if the New South Wales government's confidence in its public health contact-tracing system was justified against the new Delta variant of Covid-19. Yet when the virus found a home in poorer suburbs such as Fairfield, where more than half the residents were born overseas, it soon overwhelmed that part of the city, sending Sydney into a lengthy lockdown. Thousands were hospitalised, and many hundreds died.

The virus was not classist or racist. It had no personality, intelligence, or malevolent design. The people of Sydney's south-west and west, who ended up dying in far greater numbers than those in the east and the north, had no innate susceptibility to Covid-19. They were not worse people, lacking in personal responsibility or social solidarity, as some suggested. Rather, the virus exposed what none of us in Australia much like to talk about: inequality and class, the often-hidden or glossed-over fissures of our society. Our ability to respond to the virus—and to protect ourselves and others from illness and death—was heavily influenced by our economic position. It was reflected in something as simple as how far people had to travel to work. In wealthier parts of our major cities, people were able to spend more time at home and to travel to work significantly less, according to data that tracked people's movement.

The residents in the south-west and west of the city were far more likely to work in a warehouse, drive a truck, or provide care than those in the wealthy enclaves in the east or the north of the city. They were even policed differently from people in the wealthier parts of Sydney, facing far tighter restrictions. They were living the reality of Australia's long-running social experiment of subjecting one-quarter to one-third of its working population to insecure work, and, in more recent times, to the gig economy.

In March 2020, at the start of the pandemic, there was observed in Victoria a trend that was almost identical to what later occurred in Sydney. When wealthy travellers first brought the virus back from the ski-fields of Aspen in the United States to Melbourne's expensive playground on the Mornington Peninsula, the virus failed to take root. It burnt out within weeks. But by the middle of the same year, after escaping from hotel quarantine, the virus found a more receptive home and ripped through Melbourne's working-class west and north, requiring a lengthy

city-wide lockdown to control it. It spread from security guards
to their families in suburbs where often young migrant families
juggle multiple jobs. It got into crammed meatworks facilities,
which are mostly located in the same areas, and spread to aged
care, where casual, low-paid workers—often employed through
labour-hire firms—are likely to have brought it in, and then
worked across numerous homes.

In late July 2020, Melbourne was nearing the peak of its
deadly second Covid-19 wave, and was partway through the long,
bleak winter lockdown of its five million people. The death toll
was rising as Melbourne's nursing homes were becoming overrun
with this new plague, for which there was not yet a vaccine. Of
Melbourne's five most disadvantaged municipalities, four had the
most active Covid-19 cases. However, as state government data
showed, in much of the wealthier parts of the city, few got sick
or died. Cases were as much as ten times higher in Brimbank in
Melbourne's west than in Glen Eira in the wealthy inner south-
east.

Lockdown was grim and boring wherever you were. Those who
could work from home were sitting at makeshift desks, churning
through their daily tasks on laptops. The main fear of illness—for
people like me, who were able to work from home—was going
to the shops and becoming infected. It was relatively low risk. It
was, of course, hard for people who had to care for kids at home,
or who missed their family. Many were isolated, whether it was
the young from friends and their networks, or the old who were
often forced to live almost-solitary lives. It was often a distressing
experience. Yet the experience was not the same for everyone.
Across the city, other people had to make different, harder choices.

In July 2020, I spoke with Munir, a worker at an industrial
laundry at Spotless in Dandenong, in Melbourne's south-east.
At his work there had been a small but growing outbreak of

Covid-19 cases. Munir was a migrant with poor English, and if we'd published his real name in *The Sunday Age*, almost certainly he would have lost his job. But what he said was clear. 'Do we stand up for our rights, or do we worry about income?' It was the same question for hundreds of thousands of workers in Melbourne's working-class suburbs in the west, north, and south-east. It had been a similar tale across the world, where the pandemic, in terms of loss of human life and social upheaval, had been in overall terms far more devastating than in Australia. But the trend, both overseas and here, was similar: those with the least were affected the most.

Cleaners, delivery drivers, nurses, medical staff, meat workers, and those who had jobs that could be only done in person were most exposed. They were also the people who tended to have the weakest workplace rights, to be on a precarious contract, to be a gig worker, in labour hire, or a casual. If they didn't turn up to work, there might not have been a shift for them the next day. At the Spotless laundry, workers such as Munir were sifting through the soiled sheets of Covid-19 patients that had been sent in from aged care centres and hospitals. The sheets would move down conveyor belts to be washed and dried in giant machines. 'Most of us are the only breadwinners in the family,' Munir told me. 'We must work.'

Some of the workers had started to get sick at the Spotless laundry (although probably not from handling the sheets). Several of the workers told me the fear was palpable in the confined spaces in which they laboured. Many of the workers—largely migrants and women—lived in extended families. If they got sick at work, they'd take the virus home and potentially put their loved ones in danger. Their work was vital in a pandemic; without it, hospitals and nursing homes would struggle to operate.

For their labour, these workers were paid the minimum award

wage—$20 to $25 an hour, depending on whether they were permament or casual. Many felt the strain intensely. They could not afford not to work, but nor did they want others to get sick, including their loved ones. Some were close to walking out in revolt. Munir said they were warned by Spotless management that there would be 'consequences' if they stopped work. 'We made it clear that we do not want to transport the virus to our families. All of us are from different cultural backgrounds, and we live in extended families. We have family members who are in the risk groups.'

Another Spotless worker told me that the calculations made around risk varied, based on whether they were a permanent or casual worker. 'A lot of the permanent workers were prepared to take on the sacrifice,' she said. 'Of not being paid, to keep families safe. A lot of casual employees don't have that choice.' Spotless is a famous corporate name in Australia, its history entwined with the evolution of Australian business from the post-war period into the current era. Set up as a small dry-cleaning business in the 1940s, it had over time enriched its founding family, the McMullins, who listed it on the stock exchange in the 1950s. By 2012 it had been sold to a private equity firm. That was how the private equity model typically worked: buy an old business, load it with debt, cut costs aggressively, and then flick it on a few years later. There was no room for sentimentality or for lingering, paternalistic, familial obligations to the staff. It was the ruthlessly efficient business model of our neo-liberal times, supercharging returns for its wealthy investors.

Spotless itself had re-listed on the stock market after just a few years' ownership by private equity firm Pacific Equity Partners, which had bought it for $1.1 billion. In 2017, its ownership changed again, this time to engineering firm Downer EDI. As the pandemic raged around them, workers were offered $50 gift cards to keep working. As many as thirty-five of them refused to do so. Spotless claimed this was an unlawful strike led by the United Workers Union (UWU), and even took the case to the Fair Work Commission. If Spotless had won that case, stopping work for safety reasons during the pandemic would have been deemed unlawful—a bitter, potentially far-reaching precedent. In the end, no decision had to be made by the workplace tribunal. Victoria's Department of Health and Human Services ended up shutting down the entire laundry for two weeks. The company, for its part, told me that it decided to offer the cards in recognition of their workers' 'commitment during a challenging time' and as a 'demonstration of Spotless' values of Zero Harm (safety), Delivery, Relationships, Thought Leadership'. It was unclear to me what that jumble of words meant.

Yet the message sent to workers from the $50 gift card offer was clear. 'For the workers who stood up for their safety, it's an awful thing to hear that was the price for Spotless of them and their families,' a worker told me. And it wasn't a shortage of value in the business that led management to offer people a paltry sum to risk their lives in Melbourne's most disadvantaged area. Within months, Spotless sold most of its laundry business, which included the Dandenong site where Munir and his colleagues worked, for $155 million to a new private equity buyer.

It wasn't just Spotless workers who grappled with risking their health for a low-paid job. Many hundreds of workers walked off the job in 2020 at up to a dozen warehouses in Victoria run by big corporations, ranging from Toll to Chemist Warehouse. 'They're only doing the absolute minimum,' a Woolworths warehouse worker at Laverton told me about his employer's response to the pandemic. He had found that there had been a Covid case partway through his shift, after workers had noticed deep cleaning going on the night before. There was no message from management. 'I live in an apartment complex with twenty-two floors and 1,000 people. I didn't want to get it and spread it to this whole building.' This mini wave of militancy was unusual. Behind it was the UWU, formed out of the merger of United Voice and the National Union of Workers the year before. Warehouses were a stronghold of the old NUW, a mid-sized union with a tradition of militancy, particularly in Victoria. The walk-offs were successful in pushing back against demands from business and industry lobby groups for the economy to stay open. They likely played a role in slowing workplace transmission of the virus.

The mini-strike wave in Melbourne in 2020 proved to be an island of rebellion in a sea of acquiescence. As the virus raged across Sydney and Melbourne in 2021, there was little to no industrial activity and few walk-offs, despite workplaces being a cause of virus spread and a clear risk to safety. Workers in western Sydney instead were heavily monitored, with some required to get Covid-19 tests before they left their local area, while whole local government areas in the west and south-west were subject to curfew. Pressure and monitoring was most sternly applied to workers, rather than to employers.

In Victoria, much of the economy was put on life support. A migrant on low wages in a meatworks, a warehouse worker at a major distribution centre, or a rider delivering a meal during the pandemic: without these workers the economy and society would start to break down. But they were among the worst-paid in Australia, and all this work had to be done in person. Often, the pay or job security was so poor that workers would supplement an income with a second or third job, adding to the risk of the virus spreading between workplaces.

The subdued official response said much about both the nature of work in contemporary Australia and the nature of power. Since the previous recession, in the early 1990s, the power imbalance in Australia's political economy had shifted even further. The long, almost unparalleled, boom did much to lift living standards, and created new classes of wealth linked to property and financialisation. There were many winners as the increase in the values of shares and housing far outstripped wages. The evidence of growing disparities was clear, whether it was the share of national income going to capital, wages growth, wealth inequality, or even the number of strikes. It was not by accident. Over several decades, economic restructuring had largely favoured business over labour through deregulation, privatisation, and weaker labour laws. All the trends were going in the same direction, allowing stronger returns on capital. The subsequent rise in inequality was inevitable.

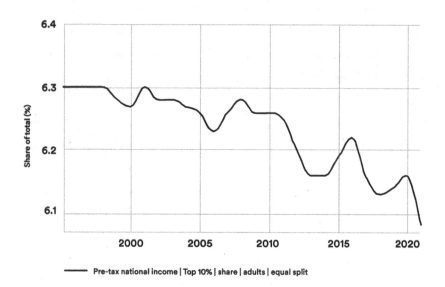

Bottom 50% net personal wealth share, Australia, 1995–2021

Share of total (%)

— Pre-tax national income | Top 10% | share | adults | equal split

GRAPH FOUR *Source: World Inequality Database*

The inequality expressed itself in other ways. During the pandemic, the value of assets rose at an even quicker rate as the

Reserve Bank slashed interest rates to stimulate the economy. The tactic worked, but it also led to sharp house price increases in what became a tax-free gift, often to the already well off. A typical house in Sydney rose in value by $843 a day in the middle of the pandemic; the median value increased to $1.3 million, up by $308,000 in a year. In Melbourne, it rose by $473 a day. This exacerbated the long-term trend of home-ownership levels dropping. In the mid-1990s, 71.4 per cent of Australians owned their own home. That level had already fallen to 66.5 per cent by 2018, with far lower ownership rates among younger people. For those aged 25 to 34, home-ownership rates were down from 52 per cent to 37 per cent over that same period, with a similar level of decline for 35-to-44-year-olds.

The bank of Mum and Dad, as it's known in Australia, has become the country's ninth-biggest residential mortgage lender, with $34 billion in loans, according to one researcher. The link between effort and reward—work hard and you can have your own home, which has been central to meritocratic liberal ideals—has been all but severed. Property ownership is almost becoming a birthright for the more privileged classes. This is a radical departure from the recent past. Additionally, Australia's tax laws—which encourage tax write-offs for landlords—have helped create a powerful political constituency of small investors resistant to pro-tenant changes. Between 1995 and 2018 there was significant growth in renters in private housing, up from 18 per cent of households to 27 per cent. Public housing renting nearly halved to 3.1 per cent as government investment in the sector collapsed.

The burden of deregulation, de-unionisation, and shifting economic patterns meant that millions were stuck in what economist Guy Standing calls 'the precariat', those in near-permanent forms of economic insecurity. Defining who is in precarious work is a somewhat inexact science. About one-quarter of employees are engaged in jobs that don't provide paid leave, according to the Bureau of Statistics—one way to measure the number of people in casual work in Australia. Over the long-term that is up significantly, from about 15 per cent in the mid-1980s (although it has been stable in more recent times). If the rate of casual employment had held steady from the 1980s to now, there would be one million fewer people working in casual jobs today. As well, there are also large numbers of workers in labour hire, engaged as contractors or in the gig economy. About one-third of the workforce could be part of the precariat, including, before the pandemic, up to one million workers on temporary visas with even fewer rights.

During the pandemic, the numbers of people with multiple jobs hit record highs, and in some industries up to one in ten people were working two or more jobs. In total, in late 2021, there were about 850,000 people working multiple jobs, or about 6.5 per cent of the workforce, including large numbers of retail, arts, and hospitality workers. Of course, not everyone working as a casual, in multiple jobs, or as a contractor is unhappy doing so. For some younger people or for those with caring responsibilities, the arrangement can work, by trading off paid leave and job security for some extra flexibility and sometimes higher pay. But it can also be problematic, making it hard to plan a family and caring around unknown shifts and no sick pay. For others, it is also a grind; whether it is a teacher going from contract to contract with no job security, or a truck driver who is engaged as contractor, with a sideline driving Ubers or doing deliveries.

The precariat has been created out of demands from business to reduce the conditions of those with the most limited bargaining power, and has been enabled by governments. Its growth has cut across traditional, more narrowly defined, social notions of class and status to affect both a casual academic with a PhD and those with a Year 10 education. Yet, no matter their background, all these types of workers are experiencing a similar dynamic: a lack of job security, and being placed in a continual state of uncertainty. It can extend beyond work, making it hard to get a loan for a house or to plan too far ahead. It is a graphic symbol of diminished power.

'Obviously, the virus is just going to find weaknesses, and it's found a weakness,' ACTU secretary Sally McManus told me during Melbourne's second pandemic wave. 'People who are less secure are more likely to go to work if they've got symptoms. They're facing different choices from other people in the pandemic. They're not all equal choices. What has changed in the pandemic is the absolute experience of and the absolute brutality of insecure work. All the jobs that were let go were all casual jobs, because they could be,' she said. The system McManus described worked as it was designed to, making hiring and firing as frictionless as possible. After the initial large wave of sackings of casual workers, many were re-hired—and then let go again—as restrictions were lifted and then reinstated. Across the middle of 2021, casuals lost work at nearly three times the rate of permanent employees, despite being a much smaller portion of the workforce.

This lack of power expresses itself in other ways. Depressed wages, uncertain shifts, and being easier to fire are the most obvious symptoms. The choices you make depend on where you are situated in the labour market. For an in-demand professional, the experience of work—and the freedom that goes with it—is vastly different from someone in an insecure role who often has to accept intense surveillance.

Cleaner Jose from Colombia worked on some of Melbourne's biggest office towers with his wife, Ana. Instead of being engaged directly, he was told to get an ABN and that he was a contractor. He had none of the basic workplace rights an employee would have had. Yet Jose told me he wore a company uniform, had a single employer, recorded his hours, and was paid $17 an hour, well below the legal minimum rate. He and Ana were tracked by a GPS app they had to use on their own phones while at work. After inquiring about her pay, Ana was laid off. 'They told her she would get sent back to Colombia,' Jose said. Their work performance was tracked by pictures they took of their own labour and uploaded to WhatsApp. 'We had to send pictures of the [cleaning] job, of everything,' Jose told me.

It is not an unusual experience. Researcher and unionist Lauren Kelly is doing a PhD on workplace surveillance and how it is used to monitor and control workers. 'In my experience talking to workers, it's one of the things they absolutely hate the most,' she says. 'When I started doing this research, by just talking to leaders from different industries, I didn't expect that ... I thought it would be automation [of work] or wages.' Kelly describes speaking to carers who are monitored by mobile-phone apps. They're told the app is for their benefit: '"Now you don't have to email or call HR [human resources]. There's this great new app that's already installed on your phone, and you just need to put your availability into it."' Yet it comes with close oversight of every task. A carer is told, for example, 'On average, it takes people six minutes to bathe someone, so it should take you six minutes. If it doesn't, well, then you've exceeded the time for that task, so maybe your pay is going to be docked.' The technology can even determine if you took the right route to work. 'It can detect where you are via GPS, and it can lead to disciplinary measures if you take the less-efficient route.'

For workers in a warehouse, the surveillance can involve flashing lights on the floor to tell them what path to walk to save time—and money. Their scanner will beep and tell the worker where to place which item, Kelly says. 'It directs and dictates every aspect of the job, and it sets a timer for every aspect of the job, too, so it's counting down the seconds.' She says the technology does not replace human labour, but reduces its power and autonomy. 'The people are not necessarily going to lose their jobs, but their decision-making capabilities are outsourced to these automated decision-making systems.' In office environments, the pandemic has seen a surge in sales of software to track the keystrokes of workers, or to even take a screenshot of what they are working on. Jathan Sadowski, from Monash University's Emerging Technologies Research Lab, told the ABC that the technology had enhanced previous levels of surveillance. In call centres, the surveillance can be at its most extreme, Kelly says. 'They even have these new technologies now, where when you're speaking to a customer over the phone, there's these little icons that detect the mood of your voice. If the software detects that you are downcast, it will encourage you to be more positive or even smile.'

Surveillance at work is, of course, nothing new. Frederick Taylor, the American engineer, became (in)famous for developing methods to improve industrial efficiency in the late-nineteenth and early-twentieth centuries. Human movement and tasks were broken down as his 'scientific management' principles tried to boost productivity and profit and to conquer the 'natural laziness of men', as Taylor once put it. It was not all passively accepted. Sabotage was often used to combat the rule of a class of overseers and their stopwatches timing every hammer stroke or movement to boost efficiency and reduce autonomy. Now, it is often unclear who the overseer is and who is watching the apps. 'The extent to which it's automated, or facilitated by a person is sometimes unknown,' Kelly says. '[Instructions] come via an app, so you can't contact the person behind the app who is making some of these decisions.'

The oversight is about control, Kelly says, and is part of a system designed to maximise production and profits through setting often hard-to-meet metrics and targets. However, Kelly points out that, despite its ubiquity, new forms of quiet opposition are emerging to such oversight. 'People will find ways to sabotage, slow down, and resist,' she says. Nevertheless, Kelly reckons Frederick Taylor could not have 'in his wildest dreams imagined some of the ways that people are tracked, monitored, and quantified at work now'. 'I think job (in)security underpins all of these processes and makes them really powerful, because it pulls the rug out from people,' she says. 'People think, *Oh, it's a tech problem, you got to fight it with tech.* It's fundamentally an issue of power, and it's a political problem.'

The prevalence of dystopian workplace surveillance points to a loss of power—relative power—between workers and employers that forced some people to take more risks. Worried about catching Covid-19 at work and wanting, on the quiet, to go slow to avoid others? Or to leave out a non-essential task to reduce risk? With technology tracking every move, that becomes harder. Australia went into the pandemic as one of the richest countries on earth, with a large middle class and enviable living conditions for many of its people. It survived the worst of the health crisis with relatively low numbers of deaths. But fissures in society were exposed—whether it was the lack of job security of casuals, who were laid off en masse in early 2020 and again from May 2021, or the lack of support for international students, many of whom worked in temporary, insecure roles.

Economist and federal Labor MP Andrew Leigh estimates that about one-third of Australia's rise in income inequality over the last generation is due to de-unionisation, one-third to technological change and globalisation, and one-third to tax cuts. 'A fall in union membership has been shown to be responsible for a significant portion of the rise in US inequality in the 1980s … one study for Australia suggested that up to one-third of the change in inequality during the 1980s and 1990s was due to the collapse of unions,' Leigh, a former university professor, noted. 'Unions may not be perfect, but if you want a single institution that will act as a bulwark against a rising gap between rich and poor, it's hard to do better.'

Labour market economist Alison Pennington told me that shifts in the structure of the economy were contributing to rising inequality. Australia's economy, she said, had become an increasingly low-investment, low-productivity, services-heavy, and extractive-based economy. 'We have lots more low-hours, piecemeal, low-productivity, public-facing jobs than we had in our more capital-intensive past. There's also statistical evidence that shows business investment in new capital, new technologies, and tech is at a post-war low now.'

In her analysis, Pennington describes a largely unsophisticated economy—a claim supported by a 2019 Harvard University study that found the Australian economy was one of the least complex in the rich world. 'We dig shit out of the ground, sell it for high prices, it makes us look good,' Pennington told me. 'The bulk of work is increasingly in services where underpayment is rife. We're experiencing the slowest sustained pace of growth in wages on record—it's near stagnant. If you look at real wages, which takes the cost of living into account, they're flat or declining for some workers.'

At the start of 2022, amid rapidly rising inflation, workers experienced the biggest real-wage cut in twenty years, with wages growing at less than half the pace of consumer prices. Penington said that with the proportion of national income going to workers in Australia at around sixty-year lows, it is no surprise that inequality has increased. 'Since the mid-70s to now we've seen a consistent decline in the labour share of GDP. Probably from the 1980s is when we start to see the break in labour-market policy that aligns with a general neo-liberal individualised approach to workplace relations.'

Psychologically, a lack of power at work is often experienced as being disrespected—not necessarily by how you've been treated by a boss, but by the situation you're in. You know something is not right, whether it's having to repeatedly apply for contract renewals or to wait until the last minute to be told whether you have a shift. Work matters. It is a source of identity—the job you do tells others about who you are, your relative status, and how much you earn. It can give meaning to your life. It can be boring or creative, or both on the same day. It is an important part of being in the world. With a relatively weak welfare state—compared to comparable rich north European countries—Australians have relied heavily on wages from work. And the relative loss of employee power has contributed to the creation of a more unequal society.

Pennington said that the job security of many workers had been undermined as part of a strategy to reduce their power, in a response to the economic shocks of the 1970s and 1980s. Pennington points to the rise in wage theft, a weakening in the level of collective bargaining between employers and unions, and the rise in insecure work as emblematic of a much-changed world of work, especially for younger people. 'We have a labour market where around one-quarter of our employees have no idea if they'll have a shift or income next week,' she says. 'No job or income security. That millions of employees are exposed to profound insecurity, and it's accepted as normal practice, is an indictment on our labour market.'

The pandemic exposed insecurity and precarity and other inequalities. We discovered that poverty could be much reduced by government support, as happened in the first iteration of JobKeeper and the coronavirus supplement, and then could be increased by decisions to cut that higher welfare spending. These decisions showed that the level of poverty in Australia was a political choice, to a significant degree. In the areas of greatest disadvantage—for example, in the west or north of Melbourne—your chances of dying a premature death from causes such as cancer, diabetes, and suicide are already much higher than elsewhere, according to Torrens University research. It is a trend also seen in the United States, where the class gap—indicated by those with or without a tertiary degree—manifests itself in poor health and in deaths of despair from suicides and drug overdoses in large numbers.

'People know things aren't working,' Pennington says. 'But I think the problem we have in Australia is that there are generational, class, and cultural fissures underneath that deepening inequality. People are more polarised than they've ever been, in terms of their experience of work,' she says. 'Of course, the historic decline of the union movement means that while we are the most educated society Australia has ever been, with so many bachelor degrees out there, that doesn't necessarily translate into an understanding of how to make things change.'

Chapter Two

Hyper-exploitation

A 'full blood' portion of dry-aged Wagyu rib-eye on the bone can set you back $310 at Rockpool Bar & Grill. With that, you're guaranteed that the 450-gram steak has a 9+ marble score and has been aged for 100 days. 'The cornerstone of good cooking is to source the finest produce,' chef and creator Neil Perry says in a message on the menu. There are Bar & Grills in Sydney, Melbourne, and Perth. It's a place popular with the rich and well connected—in particular, in the epicentre of Australia's corporate life, Sydney. With starters, sides, and a glass of wine, you could easily spend $500 on a meal, just on yourself; and double that if you're dining with somebody else. But step back from the marbled Wagyu on your plate and the fine wine, and into the hectic atmosphere of the nearby kitchen, and it is a different scene. Before the pandemic, Rohit Karki would have been labouring in the kitchen for up to twenty hours a day preparing the food, earning the equivalent of as little as $12 an hour—less than half what he should have been earning under minimum-wage laws for the industry.

So bad were the conditions that Karki, who was a temporary visa worker from Nepal, told me he could regularly work more than eighty hours a week, but be paid for half of them. 'I slept several nights at Rockpool on a pastry bench because there was no way I could go home and come back in time. I went into depression, but I couldn't even figure out if it was a depression. I just wanted to get out, but I didn't have any choice because of the 457 visa. That chunk of my life, I used to just lie down on my weekend and do nothing. There were days I just felt like crying.'

His lawyer, Maurice Blackburn's Josh Bornstein, said Karki's situation was 'straight out of the pages of a Charles Dickens novel'. 'We are bringing in workers on false pretences so they can be abused and underpaid, and suppress the wages in the sector in which they work,' Bornstein said. Karki was among a group of chefs that I came to know through my reporting on the hospitality industry in 2018 and 2019. Most were on temporary visas, had worked under extraordinarily harsh conditions, and showed bravery to even speak with me. Typically, their visas tied them to their boss. If they lost their jobs, they had only weeks to find another employer to sponsor them, or they would be forced out of the country.

Long hours and poor pay are not new in hospitality. In his Depression-era memoir *Down and Out in Paris and London,* George Orwell complained of working seventeen hours a day 'almost without a break'. Such hours are not uncommon in Australia ninety years later. Many chefs still talk of a military-like hierarchical kitchen culture, inherited from the French, and alive and well in Australia. What was changing was that people were now prepared to speak out. In the early months of 2018, an ex-colleague of mine had passed on the details of a contact of hers from the corporate world. The contact, a senior company executive, had recently comforted a chef on the streets of Melbourne in profound distress. The migrant chef, whom I will call Lucia, had spoken of mistreatment at work, the extreme hours and stress, and wage theft, while working at a restaurant owned by the Rockpool Dining Group, the corporate entity that also owned the Bar & Grills. Soon after, I contacted the executive, and she told me how she did not like the idea that the people who prepared her food at restaurants she enjoyed were being treated so badly.

Soon after, the executive, the chef, and I met in an inner-Melbourne café. Over several meetings, what emerged was a graphic description by Lucia of exploitation, and of how her visa status left her vulnerable to it. Later, one of her co-workers joined us, providing similar information. Australia's biggest high-end restaurant business, the Rockpool Dining Group, appeared to be underpaying and exploiting at least some of its 3,000-strong workforce.

When you meet people as a journalist, you always listen out for inconsistencies or for signs of exaggeration. This helps you to make an assessment as to whether to proceed and invest weeks or even months of your time in pursuing an investigation. Lucia and her friends' stories were compelling, credible, and consistent. I was convinced that there was much to this story. A year earlier, George Calombaris, one of Australia's best-known TV chefs, had fessed up to underpaying a few hundred workers a total of several million dollars in what was sold to staff and the public as a 'bungle'. By 2019, a few years later, it emerged that Calombaris—who was behind restaurants such as Hellenic Republic and the Press Club—had not so much bungled as systematically underpaid his workers $7.8 million through not properly paying penalty rates, casual loadings, and other entitlements.

The vibe of these stories, however, was not enough. I needed hard evidence to be able to publish Lucia and her colleagues' stories. Over several months, Lucia and others provided me with staff rosters, pay-slips, printouts of hours worked, and other company documents to show how they had been underpaid across several company restaurants. I slowly worked on the stories, spreading out an array of tattered documents on my desk and becoming acquainted with a world of fifteen-hour 'double shifts' and restaurant culture. By mid-year, we were ready to publish, and sent questions in writing to the Rockpool Dining Group.

The threats started soon after. I was told the documents were likely forged and that I'd been had. Officially, Rockpool wrote that it was 'difficult to comment on alleged documents we have not seen, [and which] may be incomplete or falsified'. A company representative called and told me 'off the record' that they'd sue me if I published this story and got anything wrong. Internally, there was much sensitivity about reporting on a company involving the well-connected Perry, a columnist for *The Sydney Morning Herald* and *The Age*'s 'Good Weekend'. After much angst — and some delays — the reporting was published on the front page of *The Sunday Age* in Melbourne and *The Sun-Herald* in Sydney. It told of how workers at several Rockpool Dining Group restaurants were being significantly underpaid.

The practices breached multiple sections of the Fair Work Act. The Rockpool Dining Group, much like George Calombaris, had tried to exploit parts of the law that allowed them to offer chefs a 25 per cent higher hourly wage in exchange for not paying them penalty rates and overtime. The law is clear, though. No matter what, even when penalty rates are traded away, workers must still be paid overall more than the minimum rates of the workplace award. According to my calculations, the buy-out, in practice, meant that chefs would be worse off once they worked between one to five hours a week of unpaid overtime. Yet chefs were regularly working ten to twenty hours of unpaid overtime a week, and sometimes much more — particularly at busy times of year. The company's own staff rosters revealed this.

It was extraordinary. A major company with an annual turnover of $300 million was producing rosters that confirmed serious breaches of workplace laws, apparently so confident were they of not being caught. Some weeks, the practice pushed the wages of skilled chefs down to as low as $12 to $15 an hour—or an underpayment of up to $800 a week. 'It's mental torture,' said one of my sources, describing working up to seventy hours a week while being paid for thirty-eight hours. It was clear this was not a 'bungle' or innocent mistake. Leaked emails advised workers on how not to record the real hours they worked, while some workers were provided with receipts from the log-in machine showing both the hours they were paid for and what they had actually worked underneath. The gap was large. They were being paid for eight-hour days, but were often working fourteen hours.

The response to the reporting was immediate and significant. Sometimes, what you think is important investigative journalism sinks with little trace, and then at other times the ferocity of the response amazes you. This case was in the latter category. I and my colleague and co-author, Royce Millar, received close to 100 emails, calls, and messages from current and former staff at the Rockpool Dining Group over the next week. They provided hundreds more pages of internal company rosters and documents. The Coalition's workplace minister, Craig Laundy, meanwhile, said that the government had 'zero' tolerance for any exploitation of workers, and called on the Fair Work Ombudsman to follow up the allegations—an unusually tough stance for a union-hostile government.

After a week, we were able to vastly expand the reporting, pointing out that the exploitation was occurring across much of the group's sixteen restaurant brands. The wage theft was in the order of many millions of dollars, possibly tens of millions. The personal testimonies about this were vivid and astonishing. A former senior manager told me that wages budgets at the business were set at 'impossible' and 'unattainable' levels, and could only be reached by 'burning out' staff. 'They [workers] were treated as dispensable on every level,' the former manager said. 'They [company executives] do not care about the humanity of the industry. All that was ever talked about was the bottom line ... You were told, "You need to get these numbers." I remember telling them that the labour numbers they wanted were impossible.'

A former Rockpool Bar & Grill chef, an Australian, said he had worked up to eighty-five hours in a week while on a flat annual wage of $52,000. Another chef, originally from south-east Asia, told me he was paid for thirty-eight-hour weeks, but regularly worked up to fifty-five hours a week in his $50,000-a-year job. 'On a typical day, I would start at either 9.00 or 10.00 am, and finish at about 10.30 or 11.00 in the evening,' he said. 'There would sometimes be no break at all if it was really busy. There were no timesheets at that time, and the employees were just notified of their roster with a printout.'

Many likened their working conditions to slavery. Some chefs had calculated, with the help of their lawyers, that they were owed more than $40,000 in unpaid wages. One estimated their underpayment at $100,000. Many others did not know how much they were owed, due to a lack of records. One chef who regularly worked more than seventy hours a week without being paid overtime said, 'When I left I thought about suing them, but I was afraid for my visa to be cancelled.' Another was forced to leave Australia and return to the Philippines after she was sacked with four days' notice. 'I have been working for fifty-five hours or more weekly, and I'm lucky if I get any break in a day.' One chef at the group said their visa status made migrants vulnerable to excessive work, significant underpayment, and exploitation.

'They're squeezing us,' the chef said. 'For us, it feels like a new age of slavery.' Migrant workers were even told in writing that if they wanted their permanent residency application processed, they needed to meet a number of menial workplace targets, including basic tasks such as greeting customers. They were told they could not apply for permanent residency except through company lawyers. The former senior manager at one of the Rockpool Dining Group's restaurants confirmed this, and told me that migrant workers on visas had their status 'held over their heads' by senior management.

It was a complete imbalance of power, and it was being exploited to the full. Perry used his links and friendships to try to discredit the reporting. In one email to writers of *Good Food*, the food supplement in *The Age* and *The Sydney Morning Herald*, he said, 'Just wanted to send you the company response to that story on Sunday. The one in today is pretty terrible as well. We don't abuse migrant workers, that is just something that's not on. You guys know me and know what I have tried to do in this industry and still do.' He then followed up with, 'They got quite a few things wrong and turned it into a personal attack on me so I will probably take action, but always enjoy the support from you and the team.'

In the mid-1980s, as Labor prime minister Bob Hawke and his treasurer Paul Keating moved to dismantle Australia's protected economy through deregulation and tariff cuts, there were next to no temporary workers in the country. Australia's post-war migration scheme had been based on permanent arrivals, mainly from war-torn Europe and later Asia, who worked, often, as cheap labour in the growing factories of a fast-industrialising country. They suffered from racism and discrimination, but, with relatively high levels of income equality and unionisation prevailing, they also had an ability to link with others and to improve their lot in society. Often, these migrants—and later their children and grandchildren—thrived. Yet, through a variety of small and large policy and visa changes since that time, Australia has transformed its migration program. As recently as 2006, then Liberal treasurer Peter Costello could claim, 'We've never been a country where we bring you in and ship you out. I don't think Australia will be a guest-worker country, and I don't think Australians want to see that.'

It was not really true when Costello said it back then, with progress towards a guest-worker program already well underway within his own government. Soon after John Howard was elected as prime minister in 1996, the controversial 457 temporary work visa was introduced. Now, a generation later, the model of widescale temporary labour is well established. The growth in the higher-education industry has been important to the change, as students have been drawn here in large numbers, making the sector one of Australia's top export earners. The students, increasingly drawn from lower-income countries and backgrounds, have usually had to support themselves while studying here. Some of the newer international students do not attend universities but rather private colleges, some of which have run sham courses and operated as path-to-residency factories. These students have become a source of cheap labour for local employers in industries as diverse as construction, retail, hospitality, and agriculture.

By the end of 2014, there were about 750,000 people living in Australia with temporary work rights. By the start of the pandemic, there were more than one million—a potential source of labour equating to just under 10 per cent of the entire Australian workforce. Some were skilled workers, but many were on visas that restricted their hours or tied them to their employer. As what happened at the Rockpool Dining Group later showed, this could give employers significant power over them.

In mid-2015, one of the most graphic exposés of wage theft of migrant workers was reported by Fairfax and the ABC's *Four Corners* program. The reporting, led by Adele Ferguson, exposed how the 7-Eleven convenience chain, through its vast network of franchisee stores, was paying many of its employees half the minimum award rate. The reporting uncovered the systemic underpayment of wages. and the doctoring of pay records to hide this practice. Stories abounded of workers, such as Pranay Alawala, being underpaid at every 7-Eleven store they worked in. After confronting his boss about underpayment, he was sent a legal letter threatening to report him to the immigration department for working more than twenty hours a week—a breach of his student visa conditions. Other workers described being paid at half rate, and of even being required to pay for petrol stolen by customers from the store on their watch.

Economists talk about the 'reserve wage', a pay rate below which people will not work because they have other options, whether it is finding another job, starting their own business, gaining access to welfare payments, or receiving support from their family. Temporary migrants, with no access to government support, and with far weaker workplace rights, often have a much lower 'reserve wage'.

In this case, under significant public and political pressure, 7-Eleven eventually ended up paying back $173 million to about 4,000 employees. Company-owned stores were not found to have underpaid employees; rather, it was franchisees. As part of its business model at the time the wage theft occurred, the head office would take 57 per cent of gross profit, and the franchisee the rest. The franchisee would then have to cover wages, superannuation, and supplies, and head office the rent and store fit-outs. There were many layers to the exploitation. The powerful head office was taking a big cut from the franchisee, enriching its shareholders and executives. The franchisee—often from migrant backgrounds themselves—could only make a profit by squeezing labour costs. It wasn't just 7-Eleven. Ferguson exposed other franchise networks—including Caltex, Pizza Hut, and the Retail Food Group—engaging in wage theft. At the bottom of the pile were workers, often temporary migrants, with the least ability to push back. The franchise sector employs more than 500,000 people.

These revelations, along with the exposure of wage theft on farms, and in the fast-food, retail, and other sectors, led to public pressure from some unions and others to restrict or end temporary migration. They correctly identified a significant problem—the power imbalances between temporary workers and their employers, and the exploitation of the workers—but offered a potentially dangerous solution. Drawing distinctions between 'Aussie jobs' and those of outsiders' gives legitimacy to xenophobia and racism. It divides people between those born here and with permanent work rights, and those born overseas and without them. It reduces the natural solidarity between people required to work for a living, whatever their background.

The problem is not migration, or even temporary migration, per se. A well-designed temporary labour program that gave people the same rights as others, encouraged them to join unions, and provided a pathway to permanent residency would not be so easily rorted. To give people who work or reside here access to welfare, and the ability to participate more fully in life while in Australia would also give a voice to their interests. Instead, the system, as it exists, is a reflection of how governments have been captured by business interests, rather than by the interests of those who work here, no matter their visa status. It has evolved from a series of decisions over many decades to give limited work rights to temporary migrants, and to so intricately tie the fortunes of a worker to an employer as to create a bonded class of workers.

As University of Adelaide associate law professor Joanna Howe told me, the problem with the design of the temporary migrant-worker programs is 'endemic'. 'It gives employers all the leverage,' she said. 'It gives workers very few options but to acquiesce to these types of demands.'

Permanently removing a section of the precariat—temporary migrant workers—would not solve the underlying problems of Australia's political economy. It wouldn't magically rebuild worker power, or significantly and permanently shift the power balance between labour and capital. It might provide a temporary shift in power, at best. It is hard to imagine, too, with so many temporary workers here as international students—which is now such an established industry—how they could be deprived of work rights. As a research paper by the Reserve Bank has found, there have been significant overall declines in the perception of job security among the workforce, with those most in fear of losing their jobs in casual and non-union work. But workers with traditionally higher perceptions of job security—those who did non-routine work, or did not work in an area exposed to intense trade competition—were also experiencing declines in their sense of job security. The perception matters, the RBA economists noted. The fear of losing your job helps to suppress worker power and wages.

The pandemic provided a real-life case-study of the effect of removing hundreds of thousands of temporary migrants from the workforce. The number of student visa-holders with work rights halved between the end of 2019 and just before Australia started to re-open, late in 2021. The number of working holidaymakers in the country collapsed by 80 per cent, and there were sharp falls in other types of migrants with work rights.

While a significant decrease in labour supply could be expected to impact wages growth, there was no wage-rise dividend for workers in other industries. Wage growth was even slower during the pandemic—less than 2 per cent a year—than it was beforehand. Of course, there are many factors influencing the lack of growth in wages, not just the number of temporary migrants. As Covid-19 vaccination rates soared and the economy re-opened from late 2021, unemployment fell to its lowest levels since the 1970s, and wages, finally, started to grow a little faster. Yet so weak was the bargaining power of workers that, despite the labour shortages, wages only grew at a fraction of what was needed to match inflation. Workers were still going backwards. It highlighted the fact that some of the problems were deeper.

At the start of the 2020s, Australia had a growing class of super-rich oligarchs, unprecedented in our history. The combined wealth of Australia's richest ten people was $177 billion, according to the *Financial Review*'s 2021 rich list. Five years earlier, the wealthiest ten people were worth $60.7 billion. The near trebling of their wealth was emblematic of a system stacked in the favour of the rich, where financial returns from those with capital were growing vastly faster than the economy itself, let alone for those selling their labour. It was the whirring, self-perpetuating inequality machine that Thomas Piketty had described. This is reflected in what happened to the man who brought 7-Eleven to Australia. Russ Withers and his family are now billionaires, their wealth having more than doubled in the years after the wage scandal at the convenience-store chain was exposed. At the top, people such as Withers can make a fortune from franchisees, who then in turn can make some money—sometimes barely any at all—through exploiting the people who work in their stores. At the bottom is someone earning $12 an hour with threats of their deportation lingering in the air.

In the frenetic atmosphere of a high-end restaurant kitchen in Australia, the staff appear much like representatives of the general assembly of the United Nations—a sous chef from Italy, a pastry chef from Brazil, a commis chef from Nepal, and others from all over south-east Asia, North America, and the rest of the world. Often, locally born workers are in the minority. Employers get to draw from this global market for labour by sponsoring workers on temporary visas, acquiring a skilled workforce and using the system to suppress wages. For the migrant workers, it can be a path towards permanent residency and often a better future in Australia. The bargain, for them, is that they have to stay with their employer for several years to get their permanent visa. Often, that means enduring tough conditions and significant wage theft.

For locally born chefs, the choices are not always much better. Having citizenship or permanent residency does not alter the power imbalances within an industry where there are few union members and whose self-reinforcing pervasive culture of success is based on the exploitation of employees. Industry legends abound of the successful chef who himself once pulled eighteen-hour days and was ripped off and abused by some former master of the trade. 'For sure, everyone should get paid fairly, but every good job I've got in my life has started with me offering my services for free,' employer Jesse Gerner said at the height of the industry's wage-theft scandal in 2019. 'That's how I've learnt, shown that I'm eager, got a foot in the door.' Of course, for every one of these so-called success stories, there are countless examples of workers who are used up and discarded.

And it's not just the big restaurants. A run-of-the-mill café or bar is much less likely to spend money on sponsoring a temporary migrant worker, so locals invariably make up a greater portion of their workforce. At La La Group's bars on fashionable Chapel Street, south-east of Melbourne, local workers were paid $20 an hour in cash, stuffed in envelopes. They were not given an employment contract, nor paid penalty rates, despite often working until the early hours of the morning. Internal company emails showed that the group—whose bars included Wonderland, Electric Ladyland, and Holy Grail—had run two sets of books, with an on-the-books system to pay staff, and an off-the-books one. Within hours of me contacting the company's owner, Keri Taiaroa, its website was shut down. Nearly all the bars were later put into administration. The group all but vanished.

Paying cash produces dual benefits: payroll tax is avoided by an employer, as are other obligations, including superannuation; and a worker can potentially avoid having their welfare payments reduced, making the theft of part of their wages a little more appealing. However, stuffing cash in envelopes is at the crude end of avoiding social and workplace obligations. Typically, among industry high-flyers, the methods are more sophisticated, bending and twisting through gaps in workplace regulations.

Guillaume Brahimi is the barrel-chested caricature of a French chef. Brahimi cooked for Emmanuel Macron at his Bistro Guillaume in Sydney during a 2018 official visit by the French president. The atmosphere in his kitchens is high-pressured and intense, chefs have told me. Contracts to work at the bistro are much like at the rest of the top restaurants, with staff expected to work 'reasonable overtime', a norm many accept to get these sought-after jobs in a competitive industry. In exchange for the 'reasonable' extra hours at Bistro Guillaume, staff would be paid at least 25 per cent more than the minimum wage stipulated by the award. But reasonable overtime quickly became unreasonable. Chefs told me that, instead of working several hours extra a week, they would work an additional twenty to thirty hours unpaid. This pushed their pay rates down to as low as $17 an hour, well below the minimum wage, and a clear breach of workplace laws. It was also a brutally low pay rate for a skilled worker in an expensive city such as Sydney. 'It's like hell,' one chef told me of working there.

Bistro Guillaume said they were 'surprised by' the under payment allegations, yet it was a similar rort all across the high-end industry. For much of 2018 and 2019, our work exposed underpayments at some of Australia's best-known restaurants—not just at the Rockpool Dining Group and Bistro Guillaume, but also at Teage Ezard's, Shane Delia's, Chris Lucas's, and Heston Blumenthal's restaurants.

Other big names were exposed, too, including Shannon Bennett (by the ABC) and, of course, George Calombaris, while billionaire Justin Hemmes, the heir to the Sydney hospitality group Merivale, was sued as part of a class action claiming that thousands of his staff had been underpaid. Staff at Merivale had been kept on an ancient WorkChoices-era agreement—the relatively brief period of anti-union laws during the Howard government's final years—which left them more than $100 million underpaid over several years, according to the claim by law firm Adero. They missed out on penalty rates and other entitlements, and salaried chefs worked excessive unpaid overtime. Merivale and Hemmes disputed the claim. 'The claim is indicative of an industry-wide problem,' Adero principal Rory Markham said. 'Employers have built empires and expanded their property portfolios on the back of employees being paid below-award wages.' The blizzard of bad publicity dented some reputations, but many—such as playboy Hemmes, who is close to former federal treasurer Josh Frydenberg—appeared to sail on almost untouched. His wealth increased, even during a pandemic that shuttered much of the hospitality industry.

George Calombaris, after his wage-underpayment bill reached nearly $8 million, was an exception. He lost his gig hosting *MasterChef*, and his business collapsed under its debts. Others thrived. Shannon Bennett's wealth only took a trim from the wage scandals: in 2020, he sold out the rest of his stake in Vue Group, the business he had started as a young chef. After separating from his actor wife, Madeleine West, Bennett downsized from four houses to two after the couple sold their Toorak home for $24 million and a South Yarra pad for nearly $10 million.

Neil Perry, the pony-tailed face of the Rockpool Dining Group at the time of the wage theft, had made $65 million in the mid-2010s from selling a large stake of his restaurant business. He'd previously said he didn't want to end up a 'penniless chef' like some of his mentors.

At Rockpool and elsewhere, many millions of dollars have been clawed back for underpaid workers, helped by media exposure, action from the ombudsman, or private settlements. Yet it is a fraction of the estimated underpayment that has gone on in the industry. Many business owners and chefs have cried foul about the public shaming, telling their friends in the food media that they've been victims of an unfair system.

Restaurateur Chris Lucas was able to claim that it was almost impossible to comply with 'outdated, convoluted, and complex' workplace laws, while saying he was worried about the mental health of those accused of wrongdoing. He called for an amnesty for employers. 'The restaurant industry is being painted as the only area struggling with compliance,' he said. 'That's not true. Everyone is grappling with it.' When Lucas made those comments to a freelance food journalist writing in late 2019, he knew he was in the spotlight of a separate investigation by *The Age*. A few days later, we were able to report, amid legal threats from Lucas, on the results of our investigation into his own business. A leaked internal audit of his business showed that in 2017–18 about 20 per cent of his staff were underpaid by a total of at least $340,000 across his restaurants, which included Chin Chin, Kisume, Hawker Hall, and Go Go Bar. Lucas, who later became a prominent critic of Victoria's Covid-19 lockdown, is one of the richest hospitality figures in the state, and had sold his Toorak mansion in 2014 for $23.3 million. In the pandemic, he sold his six-bedroom Lorne beach house for nearly $6 million. His business had a turnover of tens of millions, and some of his staff, according to the leaked audit, were paid up to $10,000 less than the minimum rate of the award. His law firm threatened legal action unless we destroyed the copy of the audit and provided a list of the people we had spoken to about it. We did not comply.

While Lucas claimed hospitality had been singled out, it was an industry that needed forensic scrutiny. Hospitality had the second-highest level of workplace-law breaches, exceeded only by the horrific conditions on Australia's farms. Surveys by the Fair Work Ombudsman regularly showed that half of all hospitality employers were breaching the law. Yet Lucas played the victim, and it said something about the zeitgeist that his claims were given even passing credibility. The food media have glamorised the industry, making household names of chefs such as Calombaris and Perry, while Lucas has been given a significant public platform.

This represents quite a change in Australian life and culture over the decades. Dining out, for most, was once a luxury. Stodgy British and Irish food did not excite people to spend vast amounts eating out, nor make heroes and celebrities of chefs. A flatter distribution of income also encouraged a levelling culture in which the tall-poppy syndrome was prominent and real. Luxuries were often treated with suspicion or even derision, but our food, over time, fortunately got much better. Post-war migration, at first from southern Europe and later Asia, helped change the national palate.

But other things changed, too. Spending at high-end restaurants by Australia's aspirational classes, who had done so well out of the post-recession 1990s boom, made some hospitality owners seriously rich. Chefs became heroes and cultural figures, spurred by media attention and TV shows. And yet, despite the fawning media, the reality of life in their kitchens was often brutal. Even the industry, when making submissions to government inquiries or speaking to the regulator, conceded it had a serious problem with the underpayment of wages. In the middle of our reporting, the industry group Restaurant & Catering Australia admitted it needed help to work out why the problems were so bad, and was working with the Fair Work Ombudsman.

At the Rockpool Dining Group, some workers had kept records of their hours in the years before the scandal broke, and one migrant chef said he'd worked more than 1,500 hours' unpaid overtime in two-and-a-half years, an average of more than seventeen overtime hours per week. After he went to the Fair Work Ombudsman with his records, he received a payout, quietly, of nearly $30,000. Rohit Karki, the chef from Nepal who said he worked sometimes seventy or eighty hours a week, including successive shifts of twenty hours a day, said that after he saw *The Age*'s reports, he complained to his employer. He was then placed on lower duties and pressured to resign. He eventually did so. After making a legal claim against his employer, his case was resolved soon after with a confidential settlement.

Chapter Three

Masters of the universe

Chris Hadley, a noted private equity investor, lived with his wife in a gorgeous three-level pile overlooking Sydney Harbour with a gym, swimming pool, and cellar. Early in 2020, he tried to sell his Mosman home for $10 million, but the pandemic intervened. He had planned to downsize to a Palm Beach weekender for which he had paid $10.6 million a few years before. But Hadley, the chairman of Quadrant Private Equity, soon enough found a buyer. Later that year, his Quadrant colleague Marcus Darville paid $10.9 million for the house.

Meanwhile, skilled chef Matthew Puguh worked at up-market restaurant Spice Temple in Sydney, and would often do dozens of hours a week of unpaid overtime. Some weeks, he'd barely make $15 an hour for the finely crafted modern Chinese dishes he helped create. Those dishes could set back Spice Temple's patrons $250 for a meal for two. In the kitchen, filled with migrants on temporary visas, the work was exhausting; the pressure, intense.

The lives of private equity titans such as Darville and Hadley could not be more different from that of the chef Matthew Puguh. But the links between them tells us much about Australia in the 2020s. Hadley and Darville, flicking a $10 million property between themselves, ran Quadrant, the firm that owns the Rockpool Dining Group, including the restaurant where Puguh had worked. Along with his wife, who also worked at Spice Temple, Puguh moved back to Semarang, Indonesia, after having struggled to make a living in Sydney. For several years they had been trying to claim back $12,000 they say was owed to them in unpaid wages from working at Spice Temple.

Spice Temple was created by Neil Perry. The chef, a brand ambassador to Qantas and a 'Good Weekend' columnist, has also become seriously rich. In 2017, he spent $9 million on two eastern suburbs properties in Sydney just after he sold his restaurants for $65 million into a much bigger dining business owned by Quadrant Private Equity, Chris Hadley's firm. It created a behemoth: sixteen restaurant brands turning over $300 million or so a year, and is Australia's biggest high-end restaurant conglomerate.

In the often-clubby pages of *The Australian Financial Review*, Chris Hadley is called a 'buyout industry legend'. And it is true. He's been hugely successful, raising billions from investors and making stellar returns for himself and his wealthy backers. Private equity is an emblem of capitalism in our age of inequality. It is where the logic of the system finds its purest manifestation, with returns to shareholders paramount, no matter what it takes. Often, under-performing companies are bought, loaded with debt, and then restructured through fierce cost-cutting. The business is then sold several years later for a healthy profit. In the United States, returns from private equity were 10.5 per cent per year over the twenty years until 2020—almost double the main S&P 500 index. Australian private equity has made even stronger returns than US private equity since the turn of the century.

Not all Quadrant's investments come off. The Rockpool Dining Group, so far, has not been one of Quadrant's best. It has consistently made losses. In 2019, it lost, according to its accounts, a mouth-watering $40 million; the year before, $46 million. But that figure is not all it seems. The business was cashflow-positive, and buried in the notes of its accounts you can see part of the reason why. At that time, Rockpool had borrowed $182 million from parties related to its owner, Quadrant. For the privilege, it pays an extraordinary interest rate of 15 per cent. No matter how poorly or how well the restaurants go, its owner gets more than $25 million a year in interest. Rockpool doesn't actually make the payments — so as to remain solvent — but the high-interest debt accrues back to its owner, and it is recorded as 'non-cash' interest in the accounts. The interest payments — which contrast with interest rates it pays on its bank loans to ANZ of 2.5 per cent — help to keep Rockpool's accounts in the red, so it does not pay company tax.

The Rockpool Dining Group is accumulating such an extraordinary pile of tax losses that if it was ever to turn a profit, it could offset the profit against those losses. It is hard to imagine it ever paying company tax, such is the way it is structured. At the same time as the generous interest payments are accrued and company tax avoided, labour costs are squeezed. Ruthlessly. This is the kind of financial engineering by private equity that creates both handsome returns and attracts big money from wealthy investors. Australia's sovereign-wealth fund, the Future Fund, invested in the Quadrant Private Equity vehicle that owned the Rockpool Dining Group. This meant it was a direct beneficiary of the labour practices that saw people such as Matthew Puguh sweat in Spice Temple's kitchens. But in the world of finance, managers and investors are judged by the returns they can get. The better your record as a stock-picker, the more you will get paid in salaries and bonuses. The returns you generate are what ultimately matters. It is the brutal, underlying logic of the system.

People who own significant capital, or invest it for others, such as Chris Hadley and Marcus Darville, are doing exceptionally well, as a glance at the *Financial Review*'s rich list can attest. Returns on capital are growing much faster than any growth in real wages, which has been negligible since the global financial crisis of 2008. Hadley, for his part, is keen to draw a distinction between his role as an investor and what had gone on at the Rockpool Dining Group. 'We are not operators of the business. However, as shareholders we are very focused on ensuring the group provides a fair, equitable, and safe working environment, and we know that our investors expect the same,' he told me. 'Like many businesses in the hospitality sector, the Rockpool Dining Group has had to work hard to bring disparate payroll systems together and manage the complexity of multiple shifts, sites, rosters, and awards. Investment and improvement in systems and processes is continual in a business of this group's size and scale, and that investment will continue with our support.'

Hadley's explanation is similar to that made by other big hospitality firms—namely, that the system is too complex, that many things are out of their control. Yet, after initially threatening to sue *The Age* in 2018, Rockpool management quickly changed tack and brought in PwC, one of the Big Four accounting firms, to do a review. Within months, Rockpool agreed to pay back staff $1.6 million for a single year of underpayment. It then expanded those payments, stretching back a further four years, which could be worth, in total, up to $10 million. It is likely a gross underestimate of what workers are owed, such is the paucity of the relevant records. Amid all the scandal and upheaval, the Rockpool

Dining Group was split in two during the pandemic, with its more upmarket restaurants becoming Hunter St Hospitality and its more popular brands forming another entity.

In many ways, what happened at the Rockpool Dining Group was a financial disaster for its investors and a reputational hit for its former brand director, Neil Perry. But the rules of the game were such that it was hard for the private equity owners to lose too badly. In the three years before the pandemic, its owners earned more than $70 million from the group from the 15 per cent interest rates it charged. If the investment had come off, the returns could have been extraordinary. Yet there was a cost to this financial engineering. If the owners had charged one-third of that interest rate — say, 5 per cent, still higher than the banks charged — there would have been much more to spend on the wages of people such as Matthew Puguh. The group could have comfortably ensured that everyone was paid the legal minimum wage. The company could have even paid some tax.

The private equity industry is well established and growing, with private equity-owned firms holding investments in Australia worth tens of billions of dollars, and employing more than 300,000 workers. But this state of affairs begs the question: who benefits from private equity investments such as these? Is this the best way to organise an economy and a society? Committed, skilled workers are exploited and underpaid, tax is lawfully avoided, and financial engineering is used to ensure that the returns to a handful of already wealthy people are maximised. It validates French economist Thomas Piketty's insight that when the returns to capital exceed economic growth, significant concentrations of wealth ensue over time. Using vast troves of historical data, Piketty's research found that the rule held true for much of the last 200 years in major nations. The interruption to this secular growth in inequality lasted for roughly thirty-five years after the Second

World War, when there was a great levelling in incomes and wealth. Part of this was due to the destruction of private wealth that had occurred during the war, and partly due to interventionist governments that taxed incomes and capital heavily. It was also a period of strong labour movements winning large gains for workers. Australia experienced a similar trajectory.

Income inequality fell dramatically in Australia in the post-war years, and by 1979 reached its lowest point probably since British colonisation, and at least since records have been kept. The Australia of that era was characterised by significantly more equal incomes than in any of the Scandinavian countries—long regarded as the most egalitarian rich countries—today. Wealth was also more equally distributed. However, since the late 1970s, things have swung back in the wealthiest economies. Conditions have reverted to being more like the previous 150-or-so years before the mid-twentieth century, with widening gaps in income and wealth. The economic crisis of the 1970s—brought on by the first oil shock of 1973–74, and ushering in the period of so-called stagflation, of high inflation and high unemployment—led to a series of policies attempting to reduce inflation that, broadly, favoured the interests of capital over labour. That was true whether it was the Reagan administration in the US (1981–89) or Margaret Thatcher's government in the United Kingdom (1979–90). The unofficial slogan of the times was 'A rising tide lifts all boats', or, as some said wryly, 'lifts all yachts'. That was as true in Australia as elsewhere, where at first the Hawke and Keating governments (1983–96) moved to liberalise the economy through deregulation and wage restraint.

The redistribution upwards was extended by the Howard government (1996–2007), which combined that agenda with significant changes to workplace laws—the Workplace Relations Act in 1996 and later the WorkChoices legislation of 2005.

Both reduced the role and influence of unions, while the 1998 waterfront dispute was brought on to destroy the role of the once-powerful Maritime Union of Australia. All this has meant that the changes to Australia's political economy were dramatic over the last forty years. The country became significantly wealthier, with some people doing exceptionally well. Property became a booming asset class, again rewarding those with assets and punishing those without. For many others, conditions stagnated or became relatively worse.

Through that four-decade period since the 1980s, income inequality increased by 42 per cent, rising during the reigns of both Labor and Coalition governments. It is now at its highest level since 1950. Wealth inequality—which is always far more unequal than income inequality—has been rising sharply this century, according to the most commonly used measure of inequality, the Gini coefficient. In 2003–04, the wealthiest 10 per cent of households had forty-five times more wealth in Australia than the bottom 10 per cent. By 2017–18, it was seventy-one times larger—an extraordinary growth in the concentration of wealth. This was also the case for those on middling levels of wealth. The richest 10 per cent in 2003–04 had 3.4 times as much wealth as those in the middle of the distribution. By 2018, that ratio had expanded to four times as large. Only the richest 20 per cent of households have grown their share of wealth since 2003–04.

Labour-market economist Alison Pennington told me that rising inequality is one of the outcomes of reduced worker power and of a falling share of the economy going to workers. 'We know income inequality has increased. And that it's coinciding with an increase in the wealth of the people at the very top. It's partly the result of a very conscious business strategy to stratify the labour market—with receipt of full-time permanent work with standard benefits for some, and insecure part-time work for others. High-growth services industries—such as social services, hospitality, and retail—were soon drenched in insecure jobs. They were the battering ram for insecure work's spread across other industries,' she said. 'At the same time, unions faced greater restrictions on basic bread-and-butter work like accessing worksites and campaigning. Enterprise bargaining was introduced in the 1990s as well. There's been an overall weakening of labour's ability to defend and protect its value, which has facilitated an explosion in wage-suppressing insecure work.'

Research by Pennington's Centre for Future Work has found that the share of the economy going to labour has steadily declined since the mid-1970s, plunging to the lowest level in post-war history in the June quarter of 2021—just 46.1 per cent. (See Graph Five.) This represents the redistribution of over 10 percentage points in labour's share of the economy going to corporations, or $210 billion of income a year. It equates to almost $20,000 in foregone income for an employee per year. Growth in labour productivity has also stopped flowing through to wages in the way it used to. There is a similar trend in other Anglophone countries.

The changes have not just concerned labour economists or trade unionists. 'The move towards greater self-employment and less unionisation is, in some respects, a shift back to the future in the nature of work,' said the Bank of England's chief economist, Andy Haldane, in a 2017 speech. 'Prior to the Industrial Revolution, and indeed for some years after it, most workers were self-employed or worked in small businesses. There were no unions. Hours were flexible, depending on what work was needed to collect the crops, milk the cows, or put bread on the table. Work was artisanal, task-based, divisible.' Haldane spoke about the shift to gig work, which can involve people selling their labour for one task or for a small number of tasks. It could be an Uber driver, or someone transcribing a recording on a freelance basis. Often, the work is available through digital platforms. It is a further fissuring of the relationship between workers and employers. 'There is power in numbers,' Haldane said. 'A workforce that is more easily divided than in the past may find itself more easily conquered. In other words, a world of divisible work may reduce workers' wage-bargaining power.' He said the lack of wage growth in Britain was due to this turning back of the clock.

In Australia, Reserve Bank governor Philip Lowe's road-to-Damascus conversion on wages involved a more modest shift in rhetoric than the Bank of England's Andrew Haldane's. Yet his intervention was important, marking a change in the economic orthodoxy. In a 2018 speech titled 'Productivity, wages and prosperity', Lowe addressed the slow growth of wages in Australia, blaming 'changes in the bargaining power of workers' and technological change, which had spread its benefits 'unevenly across the community'.

Labour compensation as share of GDP, 1960–2021

GRAPH FIVE *Source: Centre for Future Work from ABS data*

In many cases, despite businesses finding it more difficult to find suitable workers, 'wages growth has not responded in the way that it once did', the RBA governor noted. Lowe also looked at the role of technology and productivity—and differences between 'leading and laggard' firms to explain some of the problem. 'The returns to those who can develop and best use information technology have increased strongly. These returns, though, are often highly concentrated in a few firms and in only certain segments of the labour market. As a way of remaining competitive, many of these firms are responding by having a very strong focus on cost control. In many cases this translates into a focus on controlling labour costs. This cost-control mentality does not make for an environment where firms are willing to pay larger wage increases.' Lowe said that the weak wages growth was 'diminishing our sense of shared prosperity'.

Later in 2018, Lowe returned to the subject, and said wages should be growing above 3 per cent a year, at least—far quicker than they'd grown for much of the last decade. (See Graph Six.) 'I think wages in Australia should be increasing at three point something. The reason I say that is that we are trying to deliver an average rate of inflation of 2.5 per cent. I'm hoping labour productivity growth is at least 1 per cent—and I'm hoping we can do better than that—but 2.5 plus one equals 3.5.'

Alison Pennington says the RBA's position was potentially significant, with the decades-long orthodoxy that strong unions and high wages were a problem slowly being challenged. 'Even with the RBA, we have seen signs that they are contradicting the neo-liberal consensus underpinning central banks' inception about the policy tools needed to manage the economy,' she said. 'Despite their shift in rhetoric—particularly on wages growth—there hasn't been any flow-through to the [former] government's policy response. Philip Lowe before the pandemic was saying, "Workers,

go get pay increases, you should ask your bosses for a pay increase."
Then, of course, everyone's like, "It's not that easy.'" So entrenched
was the orthodoxy that when, during the 2022 election campaign,
Labor leader Anthony Albanese said the wages of minimum-
wage workers should keep pace with inflation, it became a major
political controversy.

Wage price index growth*

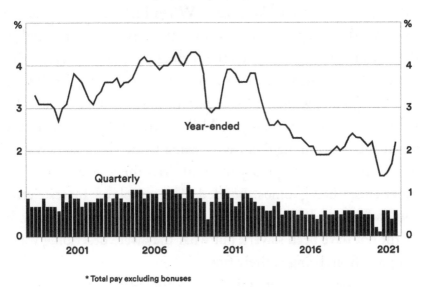

* Total pay excluding bonuses

GRAPH SIX *Accessed from Reserve Bank of Australia. Source: ABS*

Speaking weeks after the Fair Work Commission's decision
to lift the minimum wage by 5.2 per cent, Lowe expressed unease
about wages rising anywhere near the much higher inflation rate
of mid-2022. 'Three-and-a-half per cent is kind of the anchoring
point that I want people to keep in mind. If wage increases
become common in the 4 and 5 per cent range, then it is going to
be harder to return inflation to 2.5 per cent.'

There were clearly limits to the shift in the RBA's orthodoxy.
ACTU secretary Sally McManus said that the RBA and Lowe

were living in a 'boomer fantasy land' of a 1970s style wage-price spiral. 'We're not achieving 3.5 per cent [wage increases], let alone 5 per cent, let alone 7 per cent.'

When workers at the Rockpool Dining Group pushed back against their treatment at work, their complaints were not just about pay. Often, being a victim of wage theft was a secondary, albeit important, consideration. It was how they had been treated personally that was felt most viscerally. At times, workers told me they had been treated 'like a slave'. When I heard this, part of me recoiled. The comments seemed over the top when compared to the horrors of chattel slavery, the mental picture I associate with the word. I considered leaving it out of our reporting for *The Age* and *The Sydney Morning Herald*, but, in the end, after discussions with my co-reporter, Royce Millar, we decided to run the comments. Describing themselves being treated like slaves was an insight into how temporary migrants saw themselves, how they experienced being almost bonded to an employer by restrictive visa conditions. It captured their experience of lacking power. It might not have been slavery, but what they were describing was a long way from being entirely free.

These people I met and got to know were skilled workers, able to make some of the finest dishes and pastries in the country, which people would spend hundreds of dollars on. Yet they were alienated from their work, were paid a fraction of the value of what they produced, and were being treated abysmally. The underpayment was a clear breach of the Fair Work Act, as it is unlawful to pay workers below the minimum wage. But much of the other treatment occupied a grey area, potentially lawful under their visas. It underlined, graphically, that a lack of power at work is not all about wages, or reflected in the macro shifts in the economy's profit share, although they are clearly linked. As researcher Lauren Kelly told me, the way workers were treated was 'one of the things they absolutely hate the most ... the surveillance of the person at a really close level is something that people find absolutely violent and really disrespectful'.

The work of unions, no matter how imperfect, is about the only way to change the situation in workplaces where there are such power imbalances. Of course, this doesn't apply to all workplaces. In many cases of highly skilled, professional, or specialist work, it is a battle for employers to keep their staff. They tend to be much better treated and paid. Some employers take an approach of enlightened self-interest—if you treat people well, they will be more productive—and some act humanely, based on their values. The economic system, however, is dominated by the imperative to maximise and grow profit, which is particularly true in businesses owned by private equity firms. There is little room for sentiment, or for familial relations. The bottom line rules. If higher wages are an impediment to that imperative, they will be squeezed where they can be.

Higher wages, even in a situation of far greater worker power, will always reach a limit, constrained by the productivity of and the profit generated by the workforce. The ennui of work has been a feature of our working lives since at least the Industrial Revolution, and finding meaning at work or giving it meaning cannot be solved by higher wages alone. As the late 1970s showed, the capitalist system faltered at a time when workers captured a significantly greater share of the spoils, leading to both inflation and reduced employment. In the early 1980s, metal workers in Australia won a 24 per cent pay rise covering 400,000 workers, or nearly 10 per cent of the workforce. It was the high-water mark of the power of unions, at a time when inequality was near historic lows and union density at record highs. The following year, wages rose across the economy by 16 per cent, squeezing profits. Higher unemployment and a recession ensued.

The period ended, in many ways, in failure for the labour movement, as owners of capital refused to accept a lower share of profits. The absence — or even the lack of growth in profit — ended in the destruction of businesses, or capital refusing to invest at the same levels as before, in what are called 'capital strikes'. We are a long way from worrying about the limits of wage growth, but they are questions worth pondering. How should work be organised?

A typical worker in Australia can rightly say they live in a democracy with certain rights. They get to elect local, state, and federal governments, and can become involved in civil society in a variety of ways. Yet the world of work is rooted in older hierarchical forms of organisation. It is rarely a democracy. Work, as this book has described, is often closely monitored, with production done mostly for the benefit of others. There is little input into the direction of the place you work, or where the surplus goes. 'When we walk through the door to work, we're in an authoritarian state,' is how Tim Kennedy, national secretary of the United Workers Union, puts it. 'You can talk to people about being in a democracy, but where you spend all your time, you are not.' Kennedy cites Amazon, an employer whose warehouses his union is trying to unionise in Australia. In the US, the company is infamous for its union-busting tactics; similarly, Amazon has worked here, with its nascent operation, to keep Kennedy's union and other unions out. 'Amazon says we decide what's good for our people. We decide what's good for them and what's not. It's authoritarian; it's not democratic at all,' Kennedy told me.

Of course, there are differences in other parts of the economy. Some managers are collegiate and good to work for; others, less so. Most workers can still quit their jobs (without fear of deportation). However, Australia's weak welfare state — with its below-the-poverty-line unemployment support — means they would most likely quickly need another job, while the privatisation of skills and education means that reskilling comes at a high cost, too. In some fields—particularly given Australia's prevalence of monopolistic or concentrated industries—options are limited if they want to keep doing the same type of work. And often at work, unless you're a senior executive, owner, or senior manager, you will have little say about the direction of your work, its purpose.

If you're a gig worker—that is, someone doing temporary jobs or tasks ostensibly as a contractor—your employer, in many senses, does not exist. The business giving you work says you are not an employee, and you exist in a grey area somewhere between the traditional world of regulated work and the world of contractors and sub-contractors. The monitoring of your activity still occurs—you are tracked and told what to do via apps—but all the benefits of sick leave, annual leave, and many other basic rights disappear.

All this was demonstrated when a delivery driver called Burak Dogan, a thirty-year-old Turkish student, was fatally hit by a truck in Sydney's inner west while working in April 2020. Dogan's was one of several Uber Eats riders' deaths around that time, yet the company did not recognise his as a workplace death, even though he was logged onto the company's app and had just cancelled a previous delivery. The company's insurer rejected a death-benefit claim worth hundreds of thousands of dollars, as Dogan had not done a delivery or cancelled one within the previous fifteen minutes. (It had been twenty-five minutes since his last job.) Uber Eats kept sending him requests to deliver food in the hours after he was killed. It was like something from a Franz Kafka novel: Burak Dogan was being asked to work by Uber Eats even after he was killed, and yet, at the same time, he was not working for them, according to its insurer.

Gig work such as this is thought to be one of the fastest-growing types of work, although it is notoriously hard to measure.

A 2020 report by Actuaries Australia estimated that there were about 250,000 gig workers at any one time, while separate research suggests that potentially three times as many workers as that, or about 7 per cent of the workforce, regularly do gig work in Australia.

Tim Kennedy told me that there is a need for radical change to combat the extent of the wealth and income inequality spiralling out of these new forms of work and the loss of labour power. 'We'll have another gilded age that will make the last gilded age look like a picnic. How do they normally end the gilded ages? Normally, in a world war or maybe a revolution in some way.' He points to the climate crisis, the global financial crisis, and a decade of stagnant wages as signs that the system is failing. They're all linked, he says, emblematic of an increasingly volatile world unable to deal with existential problems. 'This structure is not working, it's breaking down more regularly, it's more volatile, and the next generation doesn't believe in it.'

Kennedy said we need to look at combining different models of work and organisation. 'Is this how inclusive a society we want it to be? Are we all in this together? We've got to look at how other nations are dealing with risk. Look at Australia—it's a harsh environment. How did we deal with risk? We actually were very interdependent. We pooled resources. We had a lot of cooperatives, especially in agriculture. That's a model we've got to look at. It has elements of Scandinavia's model.'

Many of us benefit one way or another from the hyper-exploitation of labour or the weak power of workers. We pay less for a meal out, or buy cheap clothes or goods that are manufactured in sweatshops in Asia. We are encouraged to experience the world as consumers, part of which is to find the best deal. Of course, there's nothing inherently wrong with finding a good deal. Yet it's likely to create significant moral blind spots about how things are produced, who benefits from that, and the environmental damage involved, and ignores what would be the benefits of higher wages for all.

Sometimes the changes that need to be made are quite small; other times, they require a radical overhaul. As part of my work on exploitation in hospitality, I was asked by my editor to look at what the cost would be of paying proper wages, of stopping people working many hours for free. Could that even work? As part of the research, I spoke to café and restaurant owners, and pored through industry reports and tax office data, to make sense of how the industry operated and what the biggest costs were. Doing the sums as best I could, I estimated that paying minimum wages at cafés and restaurants would cause some changes. But the world would keep turning. Pre-pandemic, the hospitality industry employed more than 800,000 people and had grown by a third in a decade, thanks to households spending, on average, $94 a week eating out. It is an easy industry in which to start a business, but competition is intense, and many small cafés are struggling to make a buck.

In such a competitive climate, cost minimisation is the focus. Rents are often substantial, and power prices have risen dramatically. Yet many employers calculated that they had no option but to pay electricity or rent, lest they got evicted or had the power turned off. But they could cut corners on wages, as there was so little union presence or regulation. So what would happen if all hospitality businesses suddenly found themselves paying full whack: award wages for casuals of about $25 an hour during the week, and more than $30 on Sundays? As you would expect, food, wine, and coffee at many cafés, restaurants, and pubs would likely become more expensive. There is no comprehensive research on the economic or price impact of the widespread underpayment of wages, or on what would happen if prices were to suddenly reflect the minimum wage of the award. According to the Bureau of Statistics, profit margins in 'food and beverage services', which includes cafés and restaurants, were 5.4 per cent in 2019–20. The data showed that about two-thirds of these businesses were profitable, with wages and salaries at just above a quarter of turnover. (It is worth noting that these figures would understate the industry's health, due to the prevalence of the use of cash and the avoidance of tax.)

Based on my analysis of industry cost structures, meals would likely increase in price by a few dollars per serve if minimum wages were paid. And to maintain the shop's profit margin, a standard coffee might need to rise by as little as 20 cents a serve. One of the upshots might be people eating out less often, or buying fewer coffees. Certain businesses might not survive. But it would not be the end of the world. The analysis showed that wage theft did not have to be endemic, and that food would not become unaffordable.

One thing that had to change was that paying legal wage rates had to be re-established as a norm, as the most basic of social obligations. This would require far greater oversight from regulators and unions, as the industry itself showed little capacity for change. Often, the driver of the wage theft was a rapacious owner who had risen through the same Darwinian system as a young chef. Or the high-profile restaurants had owners such as Quadrant Private Equity, with their need to squeeze out every cost, wringing out every dollar of profit. Much needs to change in our workplaces and economy to alter that dynamic.

Chapter Four

Volcanic dreams

British chef Heston Blumenthal became famous for his unusual food pairings, such as white chocolate with caviar and bacon and egg ice-cream. When he brought his three-Michelin-starred Fat Duck restaurant to Melbourne in 2014, the hype was intense. So high was the level of interest that there were ballots to get a table, despite a sitting costing $525 for fourteen courses. Once rated the world's best restaurant, the Fat Duck's temporary move from Bray in England was regarded as such a success that a permanent restaurant, Dinner by Heston Blumenthal, was set up the next year. The new restaurant at Crown in Southbank became a feature of Melbourne's dining scene, and, as one review put it, was 'a luxurious restaurant for high rollers, special-occasion diners and those who simply must tick "meat fruit" off their bucket list'.

Yet there was more to Dinner by Heston than expensive food, celebrity, and overpowering hype. In late 2018, I received a tip-off. By then, our investigation into wage theft in hospitality had uncovered several prominent examples, including the restaurants of Neil Perry and Guillaume Brahimi. Then there was Shannon Bennett's underpayments, while George Calombaris had self-reported. But Blumenthal was an even bigger name: a global star of the industry. Soon after, I met one of his young chefs, who described extraordinary levels of unpaid overtime of up to forty hours a week. She backed up the claims with evidence, including payslips, rosters, and other documents from the Blumenthal restaurant. Rosters for the entire staff confirmed the underpayment, showing that they were routinely working sixty to sixty-five hours a week, at least a third of which was unpaid. While Dinner by Heston was selling meals for hundreds of dollars, its chefs were being paid as little as $15 an hour, and a typical workday could be 11.00 am to 1.00 am the following day.

By now, this was a familiar but important story of famous chefs and business owners stealing wages from their staff. But there was a twist. On the work contracts I'd been provided with, the employer was listed as the curiously named Tipsy Cake Pty Ltd. As part of my research, I paid for the financial accounts of that company, and discovered it was not even based in Australia—rather, it resided on the tiny volcanic island of Nevis in the Caribbean. Further digging revealed that Nevis, part of the federation of St Kitts and Nevis, charged no corporate, withholding, or capital gains tax for non-resident companies on their worldwide earnings. It had no public database of corporate records, and is regarded as one of the world's most notorious tax havens. Tipsy Cake was registered and incorporated through a post office box and office suite on Nevis, and was linked to Morning Star Holdings, Nevis's oldest registered agent.

It was the same post office box and suite mentioned hundreds of times in the Paradise Papers and the Panama Papers, the International Consortium of Investigative Journalists' projects that did much to expose important details about offshore tax havens. Nevis had been described as an ideal place to avoid tax and to 'shelter assets', according to the Paradise Papers. It further emerged that all Tipsy Cake's directors were domiciled in the tax haven of the Isle of Man, located in the Irish Sea, and that other entities linked to Tipsy Cake (and the Melbourne restaurant) were run through a web of offshore tax havens in Europe, as well as through a separate Nevis company.

Further digging into its financial accounts showed that since it had opened in Australia in 2015, the restaurant had been loss-making and had paid no tax, as 'joint venture fees' in 2017 of $733,584 were paid that turned a profit into a loss. It is a common tactic by multinationals for inter-company loans and expenses to be shifted to related offshore entities to avoid tax. There was, of course, nothing illegal about setting up an Australian restaurant through a Caribbean tax haven. For its part, the company said, 'The group operates internationally within an existing trading structure, in a way that allows the business to work efficiently in its chosen markets.' The structure had worked so 'efficiently' that the restaurant had not paid a cent in company tax while sending millions of dollars offshore. University of London tax avoidance expert Professor Richard Murphy told me it was 'utterly unacceptable' in the twenty-first century to set up businesses through tax havens. 'It is extraordinary that businesses and people in the public eye still think that it is acceptable to hide their affairs behind tax haven secrecy,' he said.

So opaque was the structure that it was unclear who even owned the company. A Dinner by Heston representative claimed that Blumenthal had sold out of his business, but there was no way to know if he had, or who had benefitted from it, as the ownership of companies incorporated in Nevis is never disclosed.

We went to press with the results of our investigations, and within days of the publication of our stories, the workplace regulator, the Fair Work Ombudsman, launched an investigation. It appeared that the whole set-up had been an elaborate house of cards. Within a year—just before the pandemic struck—Dinner by Heston went into administration, and it was closed for good within months.

A creditors' report noted the employees at that one Melbourne restaurant had been underpaid by at least $4 million—an extraordinary amount of money for a relatively small business. There appeared to be little to no capacity to claw that sum back from an entity with a negligible legal presence in Australia. One of the workers, Canadian Michael Green, thirty, was owed, by his estimate, at least $60,000 in wages after having worked at the restaurant since its opening. As a temporary-visa holder—as were many of his colleagues—he was ineligible for support under the Fair Entitlements Guarantee, a government program that pays out some worker entitlements after a corporate collapse.

He described working at a Heston Blumenthal restaurant as a 'dream come true'. But the excessive work became too much over time. 'Every week was at least sixty hours ... and a lot of times it was into the eighties [hours a week],' he told me. Yet while workers such as Green lost out, the people behind Tipsy Cake suffered little. It is likely that many millions of dollars in costs, expenses, and fees were sent offshore, but only some of the details can be gleaned from the limited details in the financial accounts.

Meanwhile, Crown Casino was bankrolling the restaurant, and provided Dinner by Heston with interest-free loans—the restaurants' takings were even deposited into a Crown bank account. Crown also paid a multimillion-dollar licensing fee to Bacon and Egg Ice Cream Limited, a company related to Tipsy Cake but based in low-tax Ireland. Irish corporate records show that this company's main business is the 'exploitation of intellectual property rights', and Crown Casino in Melbourne was paying it

£1 million a year (A$2 million) in licensing fees for the right to use the Dinner by Heston name. But while Bacon and Egg Ice Cream—named for one of Blumenthal's signature dishes—was extracting as much as $7.9 million over four years in licence fees from Crown, the highly skilled chefs who created the food were being significantly underpaid.

The winners from this arrangement were a Dublin-based couple, Roger and Pauline Copsey. Roger Copsey was a senior accountant and expert in 'international tax structures', and the couple were legal owners of Bacon & Egg Ice Cream. At Dinner by Heston, everyone who was well connected was getting a cut: the Nevis-based owners, whoever they were; Crown, which gained a marquee tenant to attract customers to its casino; and even an international tax accountant, who was being paid large fees—twice what the workers were owed—for owning Blumenthal's 'intellectual property rights'.

It was another case study in how the economic and legal system in the era of neo-liberal capitalism worked. Capital was borderless, and local laws and regulations were a mere irritant. Dinner by Heston used a different business structure, but it was not unlike how the private equity owners were able to extract value from the Rockpool Dining Group through inordinately high interest loans paid to themselves and the use of extreme cost-control. Even when things went bad, it was hard for them to lose.

The other similarity was that the people who created this wealth—the workers who produced the high-quality dishes—were left with a fraction of what they were owed. For these workers, there were few places to turn. Once they figured out that they had been underpaid, workers would often go to the regulator, the Fair Work Ombudsman, to try to get back what they were entitled to. But this was often a frustrating process—so frustrating for one of my contacts that she took to recording her conversations with the ombudsman's staff to show me how bad the process was. The chef had already clawed back more than $10,000 from the Rockpool Dining Group for underpayment over several years, but the extent of her unpaid overtime meant that the real figure was likely several times larger. For someone on a visa and who had been paid little more than the minimum award rate, it was a significant amount of money that she was determined to recover.

My conversations with her were one of countless meetings and conversations I had with chefs through that period, which often included complaints by them about a lack of responsiveness from the regulator. They would complain about a general lack of help, about being told to work out themselves whether they had been underpaid, and about a lack of updates about the status of the investigation into their case. For temporary migrants, there was an added difficulty: they were reluctant to put their name to a complaint, fearing that they could lose their job and be forced out of the country. This made it harder for the regulator to investigate.

Often, the complainants were from Asia and Latin America, and other countries, all with deep-rooted problems with corruption. Their working assumption was that the ombudsman had been bribed. I would explain to them that this was most unlikely; the problems here were different, but nonetheless real. Instead of money in brown paper bags being handed to the regulator, the issue was, in a sense, ideological. The model of regulation employed by the ombudsman—like most regulators in Australia—was one of a light touch. Often, if the business accused of wage theft was large enough, it could outsource the audit of its underpayments to a large professional-services firm, rather than have the ombudsman do it. Understandably, this led to concerns by the affected workers about the integrity of the audits. (They had reasons to be sceptical. One former senior executive at a large hospitality business described to me how the auditors engaged by the business would be pressured to reduce the scale of underpayments. He said the professional-services firm eventually complied with the requests.)

The whole regulatory model is one that treats education and collaboration as being as important as — or even more so than — enforcement. As the ombudsman itself puts it, an important part of its remit is to promote 'harmonious, productive and cooperative workplace relations', along with compliance. Before deciding on whether to investigate, it decides 'whether the use of our investigative powers is in the public interest (which involves an assessment of whether any proposed compliance activity would be an efficient, effective and ethical use of public resources)'. Ombudsman Sandra Parker said that, except in the worst cases, it was aiming to avoid litigation and to encourage employers to come forward to self-report problems and to repay their staff.

In the mid-2010s, the regulatory model used an even lighter touch, with litigation extremely rare. But a series of high-profile media investigations created a strong momentum for redress, as they showed systemic, nationwide problems with wage theft. Eventually, some of the larger companies were prodded into action from complaints, or they initiated their own reviews. Woolworths admitted that it had underpaid junior managers in excess of $400 million over many years, while the Commonwealth Bank had underpaid more than $50 million. Even the ABC, the Red Cross, and much of the university sector had underpaid staff many millions of dollars. While the ombudsman's enforcement actions reaped almost $150 million for workers in the 2021 financial year — five times greater than the amount it had recovered three years earlier — it is likely that this was just a fraction of the extent of underpayment in the economy. Consultants PwC estimated it at more than $1.3 billion a year.

Not every problem is solved by using the big stick of litigation. But it is clear that the wage-theft problem was so big that the ombudsman's methods were not fixing it. Underlying this light-touch model was a view that did not account for the reality of how business operated. Businesses were acting in ways to maximise profit, through fair means or foul, against a backdrop of weak unions and declining workplace rights. They thought no one was watching and that the Fair Work Ombudsman was unlikely to take action. Originally called the Workplace Ombudsman, the regulator was a statutory authority created by the Howard government in 2007. Its creation replaced what had been a system of limited and piecemeal regulation by the federal government of breaches of industrial law. For much of the twentieth century, unions had played that role, working as a cop on the beat to recover wages, organise workers, and enforce industrial rights.

The timing of the ombudsman's creation itself was significant. WorkChoices—widely credited with being a major contributor to the Howard government's demise—had stripped working conditions, resulting in cuts to wages and making it easier to sack employees. It was political poison, and its implementation and after-effects dogged the Howard government for its last two years in office. It was in this climate—and in response to a fierce union campaign—that the ombudsman had been created, to take the pressure off a flailing government. It also pointed to a changing role for unions. In the mid-2000s, union coverage was about 20 per cent of the workforce—it has since slid further—and the creation of a better-resourced ombudsman filled the gap in one of its most important historic roles: the enforcement of fair wages and conditions.

Inadvertently or not, the establishment of the ombudsman was emblematic of the shifting of power. A key role of unions had been mostly outsourced to a government agency that regarded its role as neutral, as a kind of umpire in disputes between capital and labour. At times, the ombudsman has even played a role in prosecuting workers and unions that went on 'unlawful strikes'. That power has been infrequently used — there are few strikes now in Australia, whether lawful or unlawful — but if there were to be any revival of worker or union activity, the ombudsman's power could help slow that. Unions throughout the twentieth century had played a significantly different role from that given to the ombudsman. They had been worker advocates — not a neutral umpire — often seeing their role as part of a broader political struggle or movement, whether through the Labor Party, as communists, or as Catholic activists.

As part of my investigations during 2018 and 2019, I spoke to hundreds of chefs and workers. Usually, after hearing about their underpayment or theft of wages, I'd ask if they were a member of a union. Some did not know what unions were; nearly all said they weren't. And these were the activists at their workplaces, willing to risk their jobs to speak to me. Some were great organisers, putting me on to networks of other workers. It wasn't that they were negative about unions; rather, there was a kind of ambivalence about them. It was as if I was asking their opinion of horse-drawn wagons as a means of transport, so little relevance did unions have to their lives.

In 2018, the then United Voice union launched the first 'digital union', Hospo Voice. Pitched at young hospitality workers as an online alternative for the cost of a Netflix subscription, it had a monthly fee of $10. Over a year, it would cost five to ten times less than a traditional union membership. It introduced a website to rate bosses, and it had great success in organising protests, in establishing a presence on social media, and in gaining media attention, highlighting the extent of wage theft in the industry. Yet its model was not based on traditional union organising, which is often time-consuming and expensive. Wage-theft cases were reported to the ombudsman—in effect, outsourcing core union work to the regulator. Using mass media and social media, Hospo Voice would then pressure the ombudsman to investigate. Typically, it did not run major legal cases itself to try to change the industry's behaviour.

Hospo Voice was an important innovation for a movement that had been stuck in a rut in many ways. Yet had it got the balance right? There was a crying need to organise workers in hospitality, and there were many committed, energetic young activists keen to do so. Yet nearly all of the major cases of wage theft I exposed had come to me directly from workers themselves; they were not Hospo Voice members, and they had done their own organising and were desperate. This might change in time, but it pointed to a lack of success in unionising hospitality workplaces. This was despite the fact that workers and the union had some significant leverage available to them. Bad publicity was death for restaurants and cafés, as the workers I spoke to well understood—most people do not want to enjoy a fine-dining experience thinking that the food they are eating has been prepared and cooked by exploited labour. It was true that the industry was notoriously hard to organise, with lots of young casual and visa workers being turned over regularly, and yet the type of precarious work they were doing was becoming the dominant economic model in service industries. If these workers could not be successfully organised, who could?

Sometimes an issue can feel so overwhelming that it is hard to know how to respond to it. Think of climate change. The existential threat to life on the planet requires such substantial change that anything you can do personally—or even what a country does—necessarily feels inadequate. The big decisions are made elsewhere, by big business, by financiers, by the most powerful countries. To combat global warming there needs to be a wholesale transformation of how we live, how we co-exist with nature, and our system of economic production. Yet the problem of global warming—caused by industrialisation and an exploitative economic system premised on maximising profit almost at any cost—is not dissimilar to combating a powerful, profit-hungry employer. If we look at Dinner by Heston, for example, with its complex ownership, which was operating within a system that is rigged to favour the famous, the wealthy, the financiers, and the people who own the intellectual property, it is hard to imagine how that can be changed, either. In a similar way, if you're a cleaner at Spotless, or a chef at Rockpool, the imbalance of power between you and the private equity owners appears immense. They've mastered the game, exploiting the tax, legal, political, and industrial rules to their fullest advantage. The ceaseless drive for profit, to extract every last bit of value out of the business, makes resistance appear almost futile. But it hasn't always been like this; the system was changed deliberately to make this reality possible.

With its dark curtains, timber ceiling, and stiff formality, Morgans at 401 on Collins Street was a restaurant from another time. Owned by pollster Gary Morgan, it emanated a fusty, old Anglo-Melbourne stuffiness, from a time when the country was run by the Victorian Liberal Party and from Collins Street boardrooms. It was a venue whose best days were in the past. The same was true for much of its current audience. It was late 2010, and the H.R. Nicholls Society was honouring its retiring president, Ray Evans, the intellectual muse to former Western Mining boss and Liberal grandee Hugh Morgan. Evans—who died in 2014—was one of four founders of the H.R. Nicholls Society in the 1980s, along with Peter Costello, who later became

federal treasurer. The society took its name from an otherwise
obscure Tasmanian newspaper editor, H.R. Nicholls, who in
1911 was charged with contempt of court for calling Justice
Higgins—who had delivered the famous *Harvester* living-wage
decision—a 'political judge'. Nicholls was forced to apologise to
the High Court for his comments.

The grouping was part of the 'New Right' in Australia and
the neo-liberal movement sweeping the Anglo-dominated world
in the United Kingdom and United States, inspired by the ideas
of free-market economists Milton Friedman and Friedrich
Hayek. Margaret Thatcher and Ronald Reagan were its political
inspirations and spear-carriers. Business leaders, economic officials,
and politicians implemented their ideas in much of the rich world,
including Australia. Central to the Nicholls Society's aims were
the reining in of the power of unions and the implementing of a
free-market solution to the labour market. The society rejected the
idea, commonly held at that time, that there was an imbalance of
power between labour and capital that needed to be corrected. It
wanted a radical transformation in the opposite direction.

From the 1980s onwards, the Nicholls Society became
involved in, or inspired, a series of landmark legal cases. Costello,
as a young barrister, led a legal action for suburban Melbourne
confectionery company Dollar Sweets against the striking
members of the Federated Confectioners Association, and won.
Costello had taken the case to the Victorian Supreme Court and
away from the workplace tribunal of the time, the Conciliation
and Arbitration Commission. Taking it to the Supreme Court
was about breaking the stranglehold of what Gerard Henderson,
another right-wing warrior, had dubbed the Industrial Relations
Club. The union was forced to pay damages for losses caused by
the picketing of the site. Other landmark disputes in the 1980s,
including at the Robe River iron ore mine in Western Australia

and the Mudginberri dispute in the Northern Territory, became noteworthy for weakening the power of unions. At Robe River, Peko-Wallsend chief executive Charles Copeman sacked an entire workforce of 1,200 people, so unhappy was he with orders from the West Australian Industrial Relations Commission. Copeman later claimed that productivity doubled at the mine when staff returned to work.

These high-profile cases signalled a shifting of power: the consensus around one of the five pillars of the post-Federation settlement, as journalist Paul Kelly had called it, was crumbling. That pillar, wage arbitration, had been constructed to try to resolve the inherent conflict between labour and capital, not to encourage confrontation between the two forces. The H.R. Nicholls Society wanted conflict. As the guests sat for their dinner at Morgans at 401 that night in 2010, in front of them was a copy of an old magazine article provocatively titled 'Union Busters'. The article, by journalist Pamela Williams, which had appeared in *Business Review Weekly* in 1986, told the story of how an emerging group of right-wing businessmen, lawyers, and ex-union officials had set in train a process to smash the power of Australia's unions.

At the time of Williams' piece, the union movement was close to its political peak, but was at something of a crossroads. There were limits to what could be achieved from just winning large pay rises, if inflation rose at a similar rate and living standards did not improve. Still, union membership at the time covered half the workforce, Labor was in power, and, through the Prices and Incomes Accord, union leaders such as Bill Kelty and Simon Crean had significant sway over the direction of the country and its economy. The New Right were seen as a threat to all this, and prime minister Bob Hawke called the H.R. Nicholls Society 'political troglodytes and economic lunatics'. Costello told the gathering that the two most important things he had done were to be the number-one ticket holder at the Essendon Football Club and the role he played at the inception of the H.R. Nicholls Society.

Former Western Mining chief executive Hugh Morgan, in paying tribute to the departing Evans, told the gathering that a review of the society's early papers 'reads of an Australia that is almost unrecognisable today'. It was a world, in the society's description, of compulsory arbitration, 'inflation fuelling' centrally fixed awards, and 'monopoly union registration'—issues that since 1992 had been 'buried or cremated by voluminous Liberal and Labor legislation'. 'The Hancock report of 1986 observed almost with reverential acknowledgement that the then power of the trade union movement was an instrument of the national comity and, to quote, "There has to be a recognition of this,"' Morgan said. 'The industrial relations scene today is far from perfect, as we will soon again observe to our national cost, but it is light years better than it was in 1986.'

The timing of the dinner was significant. The relatively new Labor government had overhauled the industrial relations system to replace WorkChoices. Labor's Fair Work Act had restored unfair dismissal laws, and had introduced stronger employment standards, the overhaul of awards, the abolition of statutory individual contracts, a new minimum wage-setting body, and a tribunal with a much greater role in workplaces. There was much dark talk by Morgan and others about how dangerous these new laws were. The old men of the H.R. Nicholls Society were trying to spark a revival. Guests who read that piece by Williams that night might have taken pause to reflect on how much had changed since 1986. Largely gone were ideas such as compulsory arbitration or the industry-wide wage cases that had shaped working conditions in Australia for decades. Unions represented a far smaller fraction of the workforce compared with a generation before, while strikes were barely existent. They've declined further since. (See Graph Seven.)

Working days lost to industrial disputes per 1,000 workers

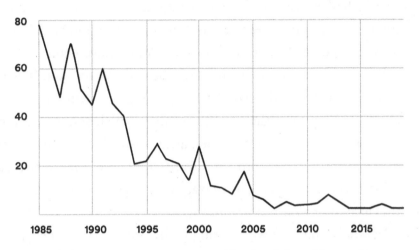

GRAPH SEVEN *Source:* Australian Bureau of Statistics, Industrial disputes data

More than a decade on from that dinner, the H.R. Nicholls Society had faded into further obscurity. There is little point to it now; all its warnings from 2010 did not come to pass. A decade of the Fair Work laws has not resulted in a union revival or a wages breakout, as those at that meeting feared. Quite the opposite. The Fair Work laws restored rights for those in standard employment, such as in permanent full- or part-time work, but even there the changes were limited. Casual work and labour hire remained endemic, while the system allowed for the flourishing of new categories of work—such as gig work—where there were next to no protections.

Union power had been almost fatally wounded. The H.R. Nicholls Society had won so convincingly that it had become irrelevant. At that time, only left-wing unionists such as Dean Mighell and his former barrister and later Greens leader Adam

Bandt got it mostly right. 'The Fair Work Act embodies all the elements of neo-liberalism,' Bandt said in 2010. 'A supposed commitment to the free market of bargaining, but backed up with harsh consequences for those who don't bargain the right way.' Mighell even made a complaint to the International Labour Organisation about the Act's restrictions on strikes and bargaining. The Act, as he noted, was no gift to the union movement.

When Julia Gillard introduced the Fair Work Act, it was assumed that it would encourage bargaining between employers and unions, and that the award system—which sets minimum pay across industries—would fade away. Instead, more and more workers were pushed onto the award. There were more than a million extra people paid award wages between 2010 and 2021, at rates close to or near minimum wages.

'We're losing, and we're losing badly,' says Tim Kennedy, the UWU leader and one of the leading thinkers in Australia's union movement. Capital, he says, has been far better organised. 'They actually have a theory, a new theory of governance, to rebuild their power. A new theory of the continuation of capital.' He says the crisis of the 1970s—with its high inflation, high unemployment, and labour's record share of the economy—was used by the political right to organise themselves. 'They used that crisis to reassert their power … and governments had to be disciplined if they didn't support corporate power.' Kennedy says that 'social democratic' norms in Australia around minimum rights and pay have been smashed. The UWU leader is one of a generation of union leaders who, when they started in the 1990s, saw little wage underpayment. That's changed dramatically since. 'I mean, this could be a two-generation struggle,' he says, referring to how long it might take to rebuild the labour movement.

The particular experiences of being in a union—of working together, of striking when necessary, of participating in the organic workplace processes of electing delegates and being able to have input into management decisions—have faded. Decades of neo-liberal reform have disoriented the labour movement. Some of it has been self-inflicted, but much of it has been imposed on organised labour by events and by other actors. The movement has been outpointed by a changing economic and political reality, and by the changing tactics of their opponents. Alison Pennington says that unions have been losing ground for decades: 'Since the 1980s, union capacity and the framework of labour protections has just been eroding and eroding, with the power of businesses to organise their operations to cut wages and conditions deepening.'

The globalisation of business has also had a disciplining effect on workers—part of the transformation of a semi-closed economy to one subject to decades of privatisation, tariff cuts, deregulation, and free trade. Being able to operate across countries has been a huge benefit to business, Pennington says. The economy has shifted from one heavily focused on manufacturing—with its strong networks of union members and delegates—to a service economy, with less job security and less union culture. 'Workers have been threatened, told if you want higher wages, businesses will pack up and go elsewhere. Sometimes that threat is realised, though most of the time it's not. Regardless, it's led to a significant increase in the bargaining power of businesses, who can say, "Well, our playing field now is the globe."'

Starting from the Accord years of Hawke and Keating, the process of economic liberalisation accelerated under the Howard government that was elected in 1996. 'Accessing worksites to check employers' books, and to recruit and campaign was hard, but WorkChoices tightened the screws even more,' Pennington told me. 'Enterprise-level bargaining had already put severe breaks on bargaining. Now, bosses could write their own agreements, undercutting award minimums. Rudd and Gillard curbed the extremes of Howard's IR laws, but clear problems with enterprise bargaining weren't fixed. The Fair Work Act is a litany of rules prescribing how bargaining should and shouldn't happen, ignoring the obstacles the law itself creates that stop workers getting to the table with any power in the first place. The result? The collapse of strike action and collective-agreement coverage, and insecure work has flooded the Australian jobs landscape.'

In many ways, the H.R. Nicholls Society got all it wanted: a largely non-union workforce with little or no bargaining power, and an economy that favoured capital. Its assault on labour regulations was part of a broader New Right project that transformed the economy. It meant, in 2021, that your famous celebrity employer might be engaging you through a company located on a volcanic Caribbean island. Or that your employer was owned by a private equity investor that had no intention of owning the business for more than a few years. Or that you might be a gig worker, and be told you didn't have an employer, or access to sick pay, or regular hours, or annual leave.

Yet, despite these seismic changes, worker agitation for better pay or conditions has not ceased to exist. It has morphed. For several years, as an investigative reporter, I've exposed much of the hospitality industry's record of underpayments. As I've noted, in almost every case the tip-offs have come from a chef on a temporary visa, or a local who was sick of the exploitation in the industry. One story would lead to more tip-offs, and then more stories. As I've noted, thousands of pages of incriminating rosters and payslips have been provided. Typically, the chefs were not asking for a pay rise, nor were they threatening to strike. They wanted to be paid a minimum wage and not feel forced to work, for free, for dozens of hours a week. The requests were modest, but they were coming from people who were great advocates for themselves and their colleagues. Their energy was just not being harnessed in the way that it once would have been — they were organising themselves. People such as this could be key in any future union-led or worker-led revival.

Chapter Five

Duncan vs Goliath

It was an incongruous scene. Brisbane trolley operator Duncan Hart sat on one side of the Fair Work Commission hearing room in April 2016, claiming he'd been underpaid. Across the room, opposing him, was one of Australia's biggest companies, Coles, using one of Australia's top industrial relations barristers, Stuart Wood, QC, an influential figure in Victorian right-wing politics and the Liberal Party. Joining the Coles side of the table was one of Australia's most influential unions: the Shop, Distributive and Allied Employees Association (SDA), with its own barrister and extensive legal team. The pony-tailed Hart was a student and a socialist activist who'd worked at Coles for years pushing trolleys. He was an earnest and serious young man. And brave, too. Hart was not just fighting for his own rights against the might of Coles and the SDA, but also for thousands of his co-workers, who, he argued, had been deprived of tens of millions of dollars in penalty rates and other loadings. The case would be an important step in what would cascade into Australia's biggest wage scandal.

Hart was the applicant in the Fair Work case, and was joined by the man who had exposed the dealings between the SDA and Coles, an official from an unrelated union—Josh Cullinan from the National Tertiary Education Union. At that stage, Cullinan had been doing freelance research in earnest for the best part of a year, his detailed work showing how deals between the SDA and Coles had left much of the workforce underpaid. Cullinan managed to convince a talented young barrister, Siobhan Kelly, to take Hart's case for free (with what appeared an outside chance to recover costs). The case, by then, had already gone through a number of steps and had run for months. Cullinan, while working with the meat workers' union, had challenged a workplace agreement between Coles and the SDA the previous year, claiming that it had failed the better-off-overall test, which requires workers to be paid more than the minimum wage of the award. Coles, in making a concession, lifted casual penalty rates from 20 to 25 per cent, and agreed to pay young workers more. In itself, that concession was worth tens of millions to low-paid workers.

When those concessions were won, I'd assumed that would be the end of the matter. It was a significant pay boost for low-paid workers. Yet it was not enough for Cullinan; along with Hart, he appealed the decision. At stake were the wages of 77,000 workers and potentially a pay rise of up to $100 million a year. The case ran for months, raking over often tedious details of the Coles agreement and industrial law. But, as Siobhan Kelly noted, the Fair Work Act was clear. Workers had to be paid more under a workplace deal than the 'bare entitlements' of the award. It was a key element of the Fair Work laws, designed to protect workers from being pressured to trade away basic minimum conditions, and was meant to protect workers from the types of cuts to wages experienced during WorkChoices.

Coles and the SDA—despite their massive resources—were left running a series of arguments that, in effect, conceded that its workers and members were legally entitled to more than they were being paid. So bad had the deal been that they could not argue that the pay rates in the Coles and SDA agreement paid the minimum rates. Expert witnesses for Coles were forced to claim, instead, that non-cash benefits in the Coles deal made the workers better off than if they had been paid the minimum wage of the award. Some of the evidence, including that submitted by an Ernst & Young partner, bordered on the embarrassing. In one example, a worker was only better off once it was assumed they had received blood donor, defence, carer's, natural disaster, and unpaid leave, and were also made redundant and off work, injured, for six months. All in one year. Wood, the flamboyant QC for Coles, argued that the non-cash benefits were substantial and that 'the value of intangibles is as old as accounting itself'. He said that the Fair Work Act's better-off-overall test needed to weigh all the benefits and detriments of a deal, not just the wages. Yet the evidence from Ernst & Young—absent the accounting sleight of hand—pointed to substantial wage underpayment, with a clear majority of workers worse off.

A little over a month later, in May 2016, the full bench of the Fair Work Commission delivered its verdict. It found, in effect, that tens of thousands of Coles workers had been paid overall wages lower than the workplace award—the basic wages safety net. Part-time and casual workers were especially affected. The decision said some workers had experienced 'significant' underpayment from the deal.

It was a stunning decision. Coles was the third-biggest private employer in the country. The SDA, which had enthusiastically endorsed the deal and backed the Coles case at the Fair Work Commission, was the Labor Party's largest affiliated union. It had done much to slow the progress of same-sex marriage in the ALP and in Australia more generally, and had acted as a handbrake on a range of other social reforms. Dozens of MPs were linked to it in various state and federal parliaments. The decision was also embarrassing for the Labor Party and the ACTU, which had been campaigning at the time to 'protect' penalty rates. Yet here was one of Australia's largest unions, and one of the party's key backers, trading them away for a pittance.

Hart, the trolley operator who had taken on the world and won, said that the tribunal ruling was 'as clear a victory as we could have hoped for'. He said the decision raised questions about other deals that had been struck by the SDA: 'This is a repudiation of the SDA's cosy deals with bosses.' The SDA had struck similar deals with Woolworths, and even worse agreements—in terms of workers' rights and pay—across the fast-food sector. The Coles decision pointed to upwards of 250,000 people being underpaid. This amounted to about one in every fifty workers in the country at the time.

From 2015 to 2017, working closely with Cullinan, I led the investigative reporting that moved on from Coles to McDonald's in May 2016, and then across all of Australia's biggest employers that had agreements with the SDA. The results quickly became a national scandal. At McDonald's, an entire store's rosters and payslips were leaked to us, and an analysis of the data showed how well McDonald's were doing out of the deal: some workers were being paid a third less than the minimum wage. The Fair Work Commission's reputation was on the line, too. It had been approving deals that it never should have signed off on. By doing so, it had made lawful massive amounts of wage theft that should have been struck out. All the major relevant institutions were failing low-paid workers.

In late August 2016, we were able to report our most

significant findings yet in *The Age* and *The Sydney Morning Herald*, confirming what Cullinan had long said was the case. Australia had a systemic underpayment problem. Titled 'Sold out: quarter of a million workers underpaid in union deals', the front-page article detailed how workers across the retail and fast-food sectors, including at Woolworths, Hungry Jacks, and KFC, were being underpaid more than $300 million a year. Over the previous five years, underpayments had totalled well over $1 billion.

The reporting was based on us having obtained store rosters and payslips for Hungry Jack's and Kentucky Fried Chicken (KFC), and having compared them to the workplace award. At Woolworths, an analysis of four weeks of rosters at one inner-Melbourne store showed that 63 per cent of employees were paid less than the award, about $1,070 on average per year for each affected worker. Many of the workers at the store were low-paid and part-time, earning just $10,000 to $20,000 annually. Darcy Richardson worked at Woolworths in inner Melbourne for almost a decade, and had resigned just before our investigation was published. He discovered he had been significantly underpaid: 'An extra $30 a week would have helped me save more money. I wouldn't have had to live so precariously. It's an extra 1,500 bucks a year.'

Rosters and payslips from a Hungry Jack's store in Melbourne's east indicated even worse underpayment. The Hungry Jack's agreement excluded penalties, and paid lower casual loadings, with hourly pay barely above the award. An analysis by Cullinan showed that one Hungry Jack's employee was underpaid about $5,000 a year, while others were paid 30 to 40 per cent less than the award. KFC payslips and rosters told a similar story: no penalties paid, and casual loadings below the award. Louis Ha, a former KFC cook in Melbourne's west, worked regular shifts on Friday and Saturday without any paid penalties. He was being paid less than $13 an hour when he left in 2014. 'We were treated terribly, to be honest. It would have helped me out a lot if I had been getting more pay for my weekends.'

Every agreement we analysed revealed that more than 50 per cent of workers were being paid less than legal minimum rates. In hospitality, wage theft was typically accomplished through extraordinary amounts of unpaid overtime, pushing hourly rates down to as little as $15 an hour. The workers, who were often temporary migrants, were without a union to represent them. In retail and fast food, the scam was different: the union colluded with the employers to push wages below minimum rates. This meant that people such as West Australian single mother of three Tara McKenna were out of pocket. She worked night shifts at Coles for $22 an hour, and was paid tiny penalties, despite the unsociable hours. She would have earned much more under the award. 'On $22 an hour at Coles, it wasn't possible for me to keep up with any of my expenses. I have financial hardship arrangements with the utilities; with everything,' she said.

The pattern was almost identical in all the SDA agreements with employers. Workers would be paid a few cents to a few dollars an hour above the award, while penalty rates were slashed or non-existent. Once a worker did more than a few hours when they'd normally get penalty rates, they were paid below the minimum rate. For some types of workers who did regular night shifts — single mothers such as Tara McKenna, or young people — the losses were huge.

It was hard to believe that both the employers and union did not know what had been going on. Big businesses such as Coles have extremely complex operations, moving vast amounts of goods a year, employing tens of thousands of people, and keeping a tight rein on costs. It beggared belief it did not know that a deal such as this was saving it money. The SDA dealings were not just a recent arrangement, either. As early as 2001, Hungry Jack's struck an agreement with the SDA that removed penalty rates and other entitlements, leaving the workers considerably worse off. Later, the Fair Work Ombudsman took action against Hungry Jack's and identified about $665,000 owed to nearly 700 workers. They were able to retrieve the money, as the SDA's agreement with Hungry Jack's had not been properly certified. The federal magistrate noted that the underpayments would have been allowed if it had been certified. The SDA itself noted in 2007 that employers would only pay a higher hourly rate 'when it is cost neutral or where it provides clear savings to an employer by being lower than the amount that would otherwise be paid under the award. This is not rocket science! It is simple stuff.' This was the crux of how its members, and retail and fast-food workers, were being underpaid.

As former ACTU assistant secretary Tim Lyons put it after the Coles decision, the supermarket chain would have known all along the effect of its workplace deal on its bottom line and on its wages bill. 'This is an incredibly sophisticated company,' he said. 'They make these claims with the aim of reducing wages costs. Any sense they would have been shocked by the decision—that is just bullshit.' Lyons said the SDA needed to take some responsibility for having agreed to Coles' demands. But he said the bulk of the blame lay with Coles and the Fair Work tribunal, which originally approved the agreement. 'They would know the effect these [terms] would have on their bottom-line wage costs,' Lyons said of Coles. 'In the end, the main responsibility lies with the boss.'

Yet the SDA was clearly culpable, too. It was run by smart people such as Joe de Bruyn and Gerard Dwyer, who had operated at the highest levels of the labour movement and ALP politics for decades. It was barely conceivable that they did not appreciate the financial consequences of their agreements. As our stories increased in significance from 2015, leading to rulings in the Fair Work Commission, multiple parliamentary inquiries, and eventually a transformation in the pay and conditions of retail and fast-food workers, the SDA refused to budge from its underlying position that it had done nothing wrong. The SDA used a public relations firm, Essential Media Communications, which had played a big role in the union movement's successful 'Your Rights at Work' campaign against WorkChoices from 2005 to 2007. That campaign focused on how the Howard government's laws had stripped workers of penalty rates and conditions. Now the firm was doing work for a union accused of itself being involved in stripping the penalty rates of low-paid workers.

The SDA's public relations tactics evolved over time. At first, EMC's director Peter Lewis repeatedly claimed that our reporting was not about wage underpayment at all. Rather, it was due to the SDA's opposition to same-sex marriage. We were using an industrial issue — wrongly — to prosecute our and Cullinan's support for same-sex marriage. I remember being genuinely baffled when this was put to me. It was nonsense, of course. Later, after the Coles decision, the argument shifted. The SDA now claimed that the Fair Work Commission's ruling that the union's agreement had left some workers 'significantly' worse off involved a new interpretation of the Fair Work Act. Again, this was nonsense. Previously, in a 2013 written submission, the SDA had said the better-off-overall test was to be applied to each employee. The union knew how the law worked, and its claim in response to the Coles decision was deflection. As University of Adelaide law professor Andrew Stewart, who helped draft the Fair Work Act, put it, the law is 'crystal clear': every worker has to be better off when compared to the award.

There was frenzied lobbying of my editors, and attempts to provoke a reaction from me. It mostly did not work. There was even lobbying of judges of the Walkley Awards to try to discredit our investigations, after the reporting received four nominations and two awards across 2016 and 2017. Those doing the lobbying were reportedly told by a judge 'in no uncertain terms to back off'. A fake Twitter account was set up to troll me. Senior unionists were lobbied to discredit both me and Cullinan, and years later, in 2019, the union wrote to the editor of *The Sydney Morning Herald* after a different reporter referenced our investigation. The SDA said that our reporting was a 'slur on the entire union movement … We reject the assertion that SDA-negotiated agreements have ever left workers worse off.' The letter even claimed that when we had been told about an alleged error in our reporting, we had said, 'We don't care.' Again, the claims were nonsense. Any mention of the wage scandal would set the SDA off.

The public statements were aggressive, too. One written response started with: '*The Age*'s ongoing attack on the SDA shows it has no interest in or understanding of the history of the Australian labour movement. The SDA maintains its position that the Coles EBA delivered significant improvements above the award for the vast majority of Coles workers.' The union's statement continued, 'However, the FWC's new interpretation of the BOOT [better-off-overall test] means that the Coles Agreement was found not to comply. The SDA will, as always, apply the accepted BOOT principles of the day in any future negotiations.'

Typically, the SDA's approach mixed largely factual statements with false ones, noting that retail workers in Australia were among the best paid in the world. That was true—all workers in Australia paid lawfully are well paid, as we have a high minimum wage, whether it's in fast food, restaurants, or construction. Yet the position of retail workers had barely improved in decades, an analysis of historical wage data showed. The real issue, of course, was that some workers on SDA deals were paid as much as one-third less than the minimum wage stipulated by the award. The SDA's claim was not true for young workers, either. Australia has high minimum wages for adults, but they are considerably lower for young workers, due to our junior pay rates, even by rich-world standards.

Yet, at other times, the SDA all but conceded it had problems. At the peak of the scandal—in mid-2016—Gerard Dwyer wrote to union leaders saying it was conducting a review of nearly 100 enterprise agreements in a bid to make them compliant with the Fair Work Act. He conceded that workers would 'inevitably' have to be paid more, 'either through higher penalty rates or even higher base rates of pay … If an employer does not agree to bargain, cancellation or termination of the agreement will be pursued.' Even then, the union still clung to the fiction that this has been forced on it by new interpretations of the law by the Fair Work Commission, and not by its own actions.

Joe de Bruyn was deadly serious when I and Royce Millar interviewed him as part of a 2015 profile for *The Age*. 'Marriage started with Adam and Eve,' he told us, straight-faced. The stern, long-term, proudly Catholic leader of the SDA was retiring after thirty-six years in the job. As we began the interview, he told us he wanted to talk about industrial relations, not sex and social issues. Which we did. But as the hour-long interview reached its conclusion, we asked a few questions about same-sex marriage. For the first time in the interview, de Bruyn became animated, deeply involved in the issues. 'Marriage is between a man and a woman; always was, always will be. It is based on what is innate in human nature,' he told us, thundering like an Old Testament prophet. He was dismissive of the notion that many of his members might think differently from him or the SDA, even though many retail workers are young and some would be gay. He said they agreed with him 'absolutely'. It was an objective truth, he said, that same-sex couples could not marry.

It wasn't just in interviews. The same views were evident in a 2012 Senate inquiry into same sex-marriage, when de Bruyn, in his submission, said marriage was for 'procreation' and that the push to change it was to 'emasculate' marriage and 'abolish it as an institution'. He argued that being gay was a choice, and said it could not be compared to discrimination based on race or gender. In an extraordinary passage, he even compared sexuality to being born with dwarfism: 'For instance, a person born with a disability or born with dwarfism is entitled, simply because of their humanness, to equal treatment. The fact that a dwarf is unlikely to play basketball is not discrimination. There is no scientific, medical, or psychiatric authority that claims sexual orientation to be a birth mark (such as race or gender).'

No doubt, Labor MPs, backed by the union, got a similar message. By the time we profiled de Bruyn, there was already strong public support for legalising same-sex marriage; only parliamentary politics had got in the way. It felt to me at the time of our interview that de Bruyn was describing an already vanished world, one where most of his members were still conservative about social issues such as this. He insisted that 'logic' would win and that Australians would realise that same-sex marriage was wrong. If the law changed to allow same-sex marriage, he added, it would show that the law 'is an ass'.

These weren't the ravings of just one increasingly out-of-step retiring union official; the SDA as an institution had dozens of MPs who relied on its support in state and federal parliaments. Up to one-sixth of the federal caucus was linked to the union at the time, with slightly smaller numbers in Victoria. It was particularly strong in South Australia (where, most recently, it produced that state's new Labor premier, Peter Malinauskas). The union's senior leadership appeared as one. Its influence on Labor and ACTU policy was significant, most topically at that time in its moves to block marriage equality from becoming a binding party policy.

When prime minister Julia Gillard surprised Australia with her opposition to same-sex marriage, few in Labor doubted that her stance was really about keeping SDA support for her leadership. In her memoir, *My Story*, she insisted that her position reflected her feminist discomfort with all marriage. More broadly, as former federal Labor minister and ACTU secretary Greg Combet delicately put it in an interview with us for a 2016 piece published in 'Good Weekend', 'The social-policy concerns of the Catholic Church — abortion, same-sex marriage — were always at the forefront for the SDA ... I suppose you could say the SDA played an important role in making sure the ACTU did not take a position on some socially progressive issues.'

These issues weren't confined to same-sex marriage, IVF, abortion, or stem-cell research. De Bruyn, the man whom Gough Whitlam famously dubbed 'a Dutchman who hates dykes', represented one of the last bastions of conservative Catholicism in an increasingly socially progressive labour movement. He and his union were a Cold War hangover in a movement that had moved on from the fierce Catholic-and-communist battles of the post-war years. Now the battle for the broader union movement was to maintain its relevance and, in a deeper sense, to ensure its survival. In de Bruyn, you could hear the echoes of the past, in the way he spoke, and in the austerity of his office. My family, similar to de Bruyn's, were also from a Dutch Catholic background. I recognised the foreboding style, the stern morality about what was right and wrong. It was mostly ill-fitting in secular Australia to be the Hieronymus Bosch of the Antipodes.

De Bruyn was an heir in the tradition of activist and conservative intellectual B.A. Santamaria, a man of a similar foreboding ilk. Santamaria had spent the post-war years battling communists in the labour movement and throughout society. In 1952, he wrote to Archbishop Daniel Mannix to outline the next objective: control of the ALP to 'implement a Christian social program in both the state and federal spheres'. The campaign was initially run by the Catholic Social Studies Movement, later rebadged as the National Civic Council (NCC). It would influence Australian politics through the Cold War, trigger the seismic Labor split of 1955—which helped keep Labor out of power federally until 1972—and define the post-war SDA. It wasn't just a political movement; the NCC worked with Australian intelligence in its surveillance of communists for many years. Such was the NCC's discipline and zeal that ASIO grew concerned that perhaps it was also being infiltrated. One confidential report in the National Archives described the NCC as 'clandestine,' stating that its members were more difficult to identify than those of the Communist Party. Other ASIO reports from 1973 marked 'secret' described the NCC as having various targets—unions, government departments, and indeed ASIO itself—that it was 'seeking to penetrate with undeclared members'.

But it hadn't always been this way. Once the union had been on the left, and its magazine had mourned the 'great' Vladimir Lenin and how 'the land was taken from landowners who did not work it', and described how, due to the Russian Revolution, the 'working class took control of society'. But by the early 1950s, the SDA, along with three other prominent unions covering ironworkers, the clerks, and carpenters, would be controlled by the Catholic right, and would be out of the ALP amid the seismic split of the mid-1950s. They returned in the mid-1980s as part of Labor leader Bob Hawke's bid to shore up right-wing numbers in the Victorian party. By the late 1980s, the communist menace had receded, and the four main NCC unions were back in the

ALP fold. The clerks, carpenters, and ironworkers have since been taken over by rivals or subsumed by other unions, while the SDA is the last surviving union of the Catholic-controlled 'grouper' unions—named after the industrial groups in the 1940s and 1950s organised to counter communists in the unions.

Publicly, including in our *Age* interview, de Bruyn always denied involvement with the NCC and any association with Santamaria. Even in a 1994 interview with the NSW Labor Council, a transcript of which is lodged with the National Library of Australia, de Bruyn said 'No' when asked if he'd ever been an NCC member. Throughout these interviews, he spoke as if he had almost fallen into the SDA and a lifetime of activism. Yet separate documents from the State Library of New South Wales include copies of NCC membership records from the 1970s for both de Bruyn and his long-time offsider, Ian Blandthorn (see image below). It was clear this was a lifelong commitment to the cause and of a particular view of the world.

Name *de BRUYN, Joseph*			
Address *4/94 Gillies St, Fairfield*			
	Phone		
M1 M2 F	DG		*A 2*
FC Lib Alp	S/R FTO NO VH		
R SB NCRM C E			
T Y			
(I) *SDA* *Office Manager*			
W Waa			

Little has changed at the SDA since its embrace of the fierce anti-communism and social conservatism of the 1950s. Even in 2020, amid debate about the Victorian Andrews Labor government's participation in the Belt and Road trade deal with China, Michael Donovan, the Victorian secretary since 1996, wrote to the premier pushing for change. The SDA, Donovan wrote, 'stood on the side of the Chinese' people and not the communist country's 'authoritarian government ... We played our part in bringing down the Iron Curtain and giving human rights to the people of Eastern Europe and Russia ... History will judge all of us. We want history to judge that we stood side by side with the Chinese people.'

It was a grandiose claim, on one level ridiculous—what role did a single Australian union play in bringing down the Iron Curtain? But it also gave an insight into how the SDA still sees itself, and into the power it has become accustomed to wielding. That power comes from factional numbers in Labor, and the ability to influence and control preselections. Ultimately, those numbers are drawn from the scale of its membership. Unlike most other unions, it draws this membership strength from its closeness to major employers, and not from its militancy, its independence, or its ability to negotiate world-leading wages and conditions. The SDA has provided large employers with predictable wage increases, zero industrial disruption, and a cooperative single voice speaking for a large and dispersed workforce. 'They're Catholic, they're tribal, they're anti-communist. But they do believe in social justice,' is how former ACTU secretary Bill Kelty put it. '[The SDA] is a Catholic union with Catholic connections. A lot of employers supported it because of that, but they also supported it because the SDA was a moderate and friendly union.'

That relationship was cemented with a landmark deal in the early 1970s, whereby six big retailers literally signed up SDA members. Under the deal, membership of the union exploded from about 57,000 to an eventual high of almost one-quarter of a million. While strict closed-shop arrangements are no longer allowed in Australia, SDA organisers are also welcome at, and regularly attend, employee inductions. (My own experience was not unusual. When I started working as a shelf-stacker at Franklins in 1997, my manager signed me up to the SDA. I never met an SDA organiser or delegate, and was let go eighteen months later, soon after my twenty-first birthday, when the company would have had to pay me a full adult wage). As de Bruyn described it in 2014, 'If we have a fundamental problem with a company, I will go to the top of the company and say, "You have a problem, and you have to fix it."' It was an approach that won support from all sorts of places, including a prominent H.R. Nicholls grandee and federal employment minister, Eric Abetz: 'Joe de Bruyn is a role model of trade union officialdom. He is the type of official that gives trade unionism a good name.'

When we interviewed the retiring de Bruyn about his career, he struggled to remember ever having been on a picket line. He recalled a picket over the closure of the failing Waltons department store, maybe in the 1980s. Even then, it is unclear if he actually joined it. For him and the network of conservative Catholics who kept an iron grip on the union, such as Ian Blandthorn, Michael Donovan, and, later, Gerard Dwyer, it was clear that social issues — rather than industrial ones — were what truly animated them. Greg Combet and Bill Kelty called the SDA's model of unionism a 'partnership'. Combet called it a 'legitimate' model, but one that came with an inherent danger. Unions became reliant on employers, weakening their bargaining power. 'There was always a risk this would impact outcomes for workers,' he said. The SDA is not the only union to have pursued this method. The Australian Workers' Union, also a Labor-right union, has adopted similar tactics. As Combet noted, there is a place for this approach. Progress in industrial relations is not a straight line: there's a need for compromise, to win what you can, when you can.

For Labor elders such as Combet and Kelty, there were concerns about the implications of our reporting: about how it was discrediting the SDA and about what a retail sector might look like without them. 'They [the SDA] believe that retail workers are better off with than without the SDA, and what's more, they're right,' Combet said as part of our 2016 'Good Weekend' article. Yet it was also true that, despite the union's denials, it had played a major role—as a partner, in effect—in establishing and maintaining a system of widespread wage theft. The SDA's industrial approach resulted in many workers getting paid below the minimum wage for years. Upwards of 250,000 workers were underpaid. The losses stretching back many years were hard to fathom. This was a regression so bad that it naturally raised the question whether workers would be better off with a smaller, more aggressive representative.

If this is the best that could be done, it's hard to imagine that there is much hope for the labour movement. Why join? Why be active? At 7-Eleven, in franchises, in hospitality, and in workplaces owned by private equity, the power imbalance is such that it is hard for workers to extract a fair share of the value they create. In all those cases, few of the workers are union members, which is the case for many workers in casual or precarious work. The workplace laws have made union organising much harder than it used to be.

Wages, as we've seen, are losing out to profits in the economy as a whole. The SDA's collusion with big business threw up paradoxes. In a wealthy country such as ours, retail workers, on one level, were doing well, compared to a gig worker or many hospitality workers. The wage theft, where it existed, was less than in some non-unionised workforces. Yet this was a unionised workforce that was losing badly. There was something almost worse about what the SDA had done to them: part of the reason they were losing out was because people who ran their union wanted to implement a social agenda and exercise political control and influence, no matter what the members may have thought about it. It was undemocratic, to say the least, but also exploitative.

Writer Guy Rundle described the issue well. He spoke of meeting low-wage food workers in Ohio in the US, and how they had been energised by fighting back against their employer in a situation of poverty wages and extreme exploitation. He contrasted this to the situation faced by SDA members at Coles. 'The worst deal that the SDA could or would get for their members would most likely be better than the best deal similar American workers get,' he wrote. 'Yet, at the same time, the union has turned (or did turn) into a machine for the systematic exploitation of its members.' He described Australia's industrial relations system of the past 100 years—with its history of a living wage and enviable conditions—as going 'from being one of the best in the world to one of the worst, by the simple process of decline, decadence, and elitism'.

'Thus, the central paradox of Australian unionism in its current state. When these official, cemented-in unions are running properly, they give Australian workers a better deal than most. But when they use their workers as a means to an end, that's reversed. The major right-wing unions have been revealed as so closely bound in with corporate Australia as to be part of it. The latest [Coles and SDA] revelations as to exactly how much they were sold out puts the cap on it—for years such unions have treated their members with a steadily growing contempt.' Rundle continued that it was 'shocking' how little shame had been 'expressed by Labor's tight elite network over these months and now years of revelations. You would think that anyone who had got in the game to fight for those with the least social power would have a more fundamental reaction to the news that the system has been run as a racket for years, with the lowest paid used as bait. Some of the Coles workers were part-timers on as little as $10,000 to $15,000. For some, the missing money would have represented real hardship: actual hunger, eviction, functional homelessness, and the like. It should be, literally, stomach-churning. The double-victimisation deprives workers even of the dignity and recognition gained from fighting directly for their own conditions,' Rundle wrote in *Crikey*.

Chapter Six

From friend to foe

It was early May 2015, and an email arrived in my inbox. We'd just published our profile on Joe de Bruyn, and, separately, a front-page news story revealing that the SDA had been paying $5 million in fees to big business a year. The fees were purportedly for the cost of payroll deductions when an employer processed a membership for the SDA. Yet they were set at 10 per cent of the cost of the membership—an extraordinarily large fee for a deduction that should, at most, have cost the employer a small fraction of 1 per cent. The fees paid to big employers were conservatively estimated to have been worth at least $40 million over the previous decade. 'It's just there, it's just a fact of life. If you were starting with a clean slate, maybe you'd do it differently,' the SDA's national secretary, Gerard Dwyer, told me. He said the union had been paying the fees since the 1971 closed-shop agreement struck between the big retailers and the SDA. It was important information, and revealed new details about the long-speculated tight links between the union and the big supermarkets. The SDA was paying them for members.

The day after these stories appeared, I received the email that would shape my working life for the next few years. 'Hi Ben. This is a little sensitive as I work at the NTEU [National Tertiary Education Union] as the Victorian Senior Industrial Officer,' the email began. 'I'm wondering if you might be interested in expanding the SDA pieces you have done to look into the "enterprise agreements" that are being done. I posit that the SDA has colluded with major retailers to "steal" the wages of mostly young workers through selling off penalty rates on weeknights and weekends. My line is that most of the employees of the very large retailers would be better off on minimum conditions in awards than on the agreements SDA negotiates.'

The email was from Josh Cullinan, and it kick-started a process that within eighteen months would lead to dramatic changes in retail and fast food, and for the system of enterprise bargaining. It would cast my 'scoop' that the SDA was paying commissions to big business well into the shade. The outline of Cullinan's later work was all in that email; it just didn't yet have the fine-grained detail. As an industrial officer, he knew the nuts and bolts of the system — especially that the SDA and the employers would have had to sign legally binding statements that their agreements had left workers better off.

'I haven't taken the time [yet] to get copies of these statutory declarations but if senior union officials and employers have made declarations saying all workers are better off yet knowing the outcomes see thousands of workers substantially worse off, then it could lead to police referrals,' Cullinan wrote. 'Whilst there is a value in a compliant "union", and a payroll deductions admin fee kickback, the real return for Wesfarmers and Woolworths is in the many many millions saved in penalty rates not paid. This is what SDA offers every major retailer and fast-food outlet in return for open access to recruit 15- and 16-year-olds.'

Soon after, I emailed Cullinan back, and we later spoke at length. Within days, Cullinan was working on a detailed analysis of what became known as the infamous Coles and SDA deal that had been lodged with the Fair Work Commission. Somehow, he was juggling this side work while at the NTEU. It was putting him in a potentially compromising position, offending the principle (no matter how misplaced at times) of solidarity between unions. Cullinan was of a similar age and background to me. We were both from the outer-eastern suburbs of Melbourne and we both came from Catholic families. He was smart, extremely capable with data and industrial law, and had a great read on how the SDA operated. As a young person, he'd worked at service stations, and by the early 2000s had become active in campaigns around casual work with other young people at the Young Christian Workers (YCW) movement, which had deep roots in Catholic social teaching. 'We were organising and active around casual work at the YCW,' Cullinan told me in an interview for this book. 'We started meeting with the SDA because we were involved in a range of industrial relations taskforces and things like that, and with state and federal issues.' Even as a young Catholic he was struck by how peculiar some of the meetings with the Victorian SDA were, with a focus more on God than on workplace rights. There'd be prayers before meetings and invites to St Patrick's Cathedral. The power, or lack thereof, of workers seemed to be barely on the agenda.

During this period, in the early 2000s, Cullinan was agitating for Hungry Jack's workers who were stuck on traineeship wages when they should have been paid at higher rates. He also encountered young workers who had seen their pay go down after an SDA wage agreement had been approved. Cullinan remembers being baffled by this. 'We were hanging out at Trades Hall, and talking with the socialists, and doing all sorts of fun stuff. We had a meeting with Leigh [Hubbard, the then secretary of Trades Hall] … and he just explained what the SDA is and why people in retail and fast food are fucked over. I was just shocked. It was just against the whole principle of what should be happening.' Cullinan ended up being involved in setting up a group called Shop Watch to campaign against the SDA. 'We were coming together and saying, "Well, how can we deal with this? How do we save it?" or, "How do we take them over?" There was a fair bit of fear. People were openly saying, "People get killed for this."'

Of course, the young activists overstated the union's power, but it was well known for its political ruthlessness and the energy it would expend on pushing its social agenda. At that time it was directed at opposition to abortion and stem-cell research, and at stopping single mothers and lesbians from accessing IVF. Its heated opposition to same-sex marriage would come later. This was also a period when enterprise bargaining was kicking off, which encouraged negotiations between unions and a single employer. It was the start of the SDA being able to use those changes to trade off conditions and pay for small hourly rises in rates—the shape of the workplace deals that were to come.

After the early 2000s, Cullinan's retail activism became intermittent—he landed a job at the CFMEU's pulp and paper branch, and a change of leadership at Trades Hall meant that a young-unionist group he was involved in fell out of favour. His employer at the CFMEU told him, he said, 'If you've got extra time, you should be fucking working for us, not doing this Trades Hall shit.' He'd even become a Labor candidate for the state seat of Ferntree Gully in 2010, and was heavily defeated as the Brumby government lost power. His interest in the SDA was piqued again in 2012 after the Fair Work Act was introduced—restoring many workplace rights—and the SDA cut a deal with Target. He did a quick analysis, and could see that many workers were worse off.

At the time, he wrote to the workplace relations minister, Bill Shorten, and the head of the Fair Work Commission, Iain Ross, about it, without receiving any responses.

By the time he wrote to me several years later—after the de Bruyn profile had appeared—Cullinan had moved on from Labor and the CFMEU, and was now working at the NTEU, where he'd successfully organised casual academics at Swinburne, in Melbourne's east. 'We were running these fantastic campaigns. Lots of workers are getting better off. Lots of low-paid workers are getting classified higher,' he said. 'Casual workers are getting outcomes and newer jobs, which is unheard of in universities.' In the early 2010s, the Swinburne union branch had grown from 400 to 800 members, and as Cullinan said, 'It was really showing that things were possible when you actually fight.' Cullinan's focus on the Coles deal had started before he'd contacted me. He'd spoken to the meat workers' union—which was having its own battles with the SDA over workplace conditions and representation in supermarkets. 'They sent me a copy of the agreement, and I was able to review it against the award and I was just like, "This is outrageous."'

What confirmed the significance of the wage underpayments was Cullinan's move to apply to the Fair Work Commission to access the files of multiple deals between the SDA and major employers. The files included all the official forms that were part of the legal process of getting an agreement between a union and employer approved. 'I figured they might put in place a system to stop me getting access to files,' he told me. 'I thought I'd better go and get a copy of them. I did that, and I saw that it was a commonality across whole sectors … that made it clear that the SDA was backing in the horse every time to say workers are going to be better off because of the higher base rate and because of the roster patterns that are worked.'

The sample rosters—backed by statutory declarations of both the employer and union—focused heavily on people working on weekdays, which were periods that attracted no penalty rates or loadings. At Woolworths, the sample rosters showed a full-time employee working thirty-two hours during weekdays, with a single shorter shift on Saturday. A part-time sample roster showed a hypothetical employee working twenty-six of thirty hours in weekday hours—again, avoiding most of the penalty rates. The sample rosters purported to show that workers were always paid a little better than the award, often by $20 to $30 a week, but this was highly misleading. In fast-food outlets and supermarkets, trade was often busiest on weekends or nights, and so much of the work was done at those times. If many of those workers had been paid the minimum wage outlined in the award—with its much higher penalty rates—they would have been better off, sometimes considerably, than they were under the agreement struck by their employer and the SDA. Among those most affected were mothers working part-time at night, and younger workers.

The sample rosters did not reflect the hours people actually worked, and all this crucial detail was being hidden from the Fair Work Commission. 'I already knew that these were huge numbers of staff [working nights and weekends],' Cullinan said. 'When I did the assessment, I knew that it was fucked, and it [the Coles deal] then went ahead and it was determined and voted on. It was at that point in time in early 2015, where I thought, *Fuck it.*'

A little over a year later, the full bench of the Fair Work Commission decided that the appeal driven by Cullinan's analysis—along with the work of Duncan Hart and lawyer Siobhan Kelly—would turn this decades-old rort on its head. 'That just burst it open and made it clear that this wasn't just a one-off with Coles. That was inescapable.' Later, the federal Department of Employment, in a submission to a Senate inquiry, further confirmed the analysis. It was basic maths that the SDA deals locked in much lower wages — unlawfully so — for most workers.

Once the Coles decision occurred, the dynamic shifted for good. No new substandard deals were struck between the SDA and big employers, and the pressure was now on for new agreements that would leave no workers underpaid. There was also pressure to terminate old agreements to stop the wage theft and to move workers onto the minimum wages stipulated under the award. In fast food, at employers such as KFC, McDonald's, and Domino's, the agreements were so bad that termination would result in significant increases in wages for the vast majority of workers. The employers did not want to negotiate, and were happy to stay on their SDA deals for as long as they could.

A Domino's delivery driver, Casey Salt, successfully applied to the Fair Work Commission to terminate the agreement between the union and her employer. That agreement was one of the worst the SDA had struck, with numerous conditions and pay well below minimum standards: employees received no penalty rates and no casual loadings, and worked minimum shifts of just two hours. If Salt had been paid at award rates, her pay would have been one-third (about $80 a week) higher. She was a part-time driver working about ten hours a week. For full-time workers, their pay would have been 20 per cent higher if they were not on the agreement. It was a shocking indictment on the SDA and on Domino's, too, that they had struck a deal so out of step with community expectations and basic legal standards. 'It's a lot of money, especially for someone on such low wages,' Salt told me. 'Unions should serve people; they should help people, not exploit them.'

Financial analysis by Deutsche Bank estimated that the savings to Domino's from the agreement were worth more than $30 million a year — a transfer directly from workers to the bottom line of a major business. The bank's analysis revealed that a move to award wages could reduce Domino's profit by a quarter. Redressing wage theft was now becoming an issue for investors at major companies.

In supermarkets, the situation was somewhat different. Data presented by an expert witness for Coles in the Duncan Hart case showed that 56 per cent of workers were paid below the minimum-award wage at two surveyed stores. One was a regional Victorian store, and the other a city store with limited overnight trade. The examples presented the best-case scenario for Coles, as they did not include the busiest twenty-four-hour stores, where it was far more common for employees to work at nights and on weekends. The scenarios had the effect of hiding the extent of the wage theft. But even under such favourable renditions, the underpayment by Coles was conservatively estimated as totalling at least $70 million a year. The real figure was likely well in excess of $100 million.

It was similar at Woolworths, where an analysis of four weeks of leaked rosters from one store showed that 63 per cent of staff were underpaid. This pointed to at least 60,000 Woolworths workers nationally being paid below award rates. The scale of the underpayment was bigger than at Coles, because Woolworths was a larger employer. However, righting the wrongs was not going to be straightforward. More workers were paid above the award in supermarkets than in the fast-food sector, which meant that simply moving to the minimum wage would reduce the wages of some. It was a problem that needed a solution.

Brisbane night-fill worker Penny Vickers was direct and unrelenting. She was animated by the fundamental injustice of workers like herself and others being paid less than the legal minimum, and by the system that had allowed this to happen. Her dogged, eighteen-month self-represented case against Coles was important, and she wanted award wages and backpay. Coles finally settled just as it was being required to produce documents to the Fair Work Commission that would have shown the details of how it had struck an agreement with the SDA. This could have included chapter and verse about how it created 'model rosters' and the like, and what it knew about underpayments and when. Not surprisingly, in the end, Coles wanted the matter closed, and it transitioned to a new workplace agreement that would pay award penalty rates 'at all times'. Those on higher rates than the award would, over several years, receive smaller wage increases until they were paid the same as new hires. It was a significant win. For night-fill workers such as Vickers, the new deal was immensely important, gaining them pay rises of up to 20 per cent. That could be worth as much as $150 a week more, compared to what they were earning under the deal the SDA had struck. Delivery drivers at Coles had already seen big jumps in pay—of as much as $200 a week as the old exploitative arrangements were unwound.

Celeste Ramnac, a part-time Coles night-fill worker, told me that her pay had gone up more than $100 a week after she was moved onto award wages. 'It's giving me a little more financial stability. I'm able to pay for rent and pay for other things that pop up, whether it's personal downtime, bills, or public transport, or whatever it may be.' Ramnac had been suspicious of the SDA after her manager at McDonald's pushed hard for her to join the union. 'When I went to McDonald's they really pushed for the SDA. Obviously I joined because I was a vulnerable young worker. Soon I realised, on my own terms, they weren't doing much. When you're not accountable, not transparent, I can't trust you.'

Teegan Condron, who worked sixteen hours a week in night-fill, saw her pay jump $80 a week to around $500. 'It's just made things a little easier. I've got two kids, and it helps them out a lot with their extra-curricular activities.' Similar changes occurred at

Woolworths, in fast food, and across agreements covering up to 500,000 workers. It was an extraordinary one-off transfer from business — which had been working in cahoots with a major union — to low-paid workers.

What happened with the SDA is not an argument against unionism. It revealed the deep-seated problem with a certain type of unionism: one that saw its role as a partner of big business, that was animated by its own political mission and much less by the plight of often low-paid employees in their workplaces. For decades, the SDA had been on a moral crusade, fighting communists, the left, progress, and social change. It saw itself in grandiose terms, even as having helped bring down the Iron Curtain, as Victorian secretary Michael Donovan once put it. Yet it was a union that failed workers, that was exposed by ordinary members such as Penny Vickers, Duncan Hart, and Michael Johnstone, along with activists and lawyers such as Josh Cullinan and Siobhan Kelly. It was scandalous. The big winners, for decades, were some of Australia's most influential businesses, which were able to bolster their bottom lines by skilfully working with a union that had a non-industrial agenda. It was not how the system should have worked.

Reflecting on it five years later, Cullinan estimates that the amount returned to workers from the scrapping of SDA agreements from the mid-2010s onwards was initially about $1 billion a year. Both Cullinan and I were careful with our calculations when doing estimates at that time, not wanting to overstate the extent of the wage theft and thereby discredit the underlying work. 'My approach has always been conservative, partly drawn out of the expectation of working with good media, but also not wanting to look like a fool,' Cullinan said. 'If there was ever a criticism, how would I actually defend it? Being conservative from the outset, it's beyond doubt now for me it's over a billion dollars. That's what we've returned—well over a billion dollars a year [in the first few years]. In terms of single employers, those estimates that we put out are generally conservative. The interesting thing in all of this is there really was not a single one of them that has ever put out a figure contradicting it.'

Financial analysts at Bank of America Merrill Lynch estimated that Coles' annual labour costs increased by $100 million a year after it moved to an agreement that paid award wages. This was in addition to previous concessions by Coles that would have lifted its wage bill by many tens of millions of dollars a year. Its own published accounts are opaque—Coles was part of Wesfarmers the year it started paying higher wages, so comparisons are not possible.

At Woolworths, the supermarket wages bill is part of the broader group, which includes businesses such as Big W. It is hard to disentangle what occurred. Yet the accounts do show a significant 9 per cent rise in wages costs in 2019–20—the first full year it paid the higher award rates (and once you exclude one-off costs). This was, in total, about an extra $750 million in higher wages across the group. For the two financial years before that, its labour costs, as reported in its annual reports, had risen between 3.3 to 3.6 per cent. Cullinan had previously claimed that Woolworths' management, in negotiations, had told worker representatives that its wages bill would rise 7.5 per cent if it paid award wages. The company publicly denied this. Cullinan estimates that wage costs at Woolworths supermarkets, Australia's largest private-sector employer, rose by more than $250 million a year after having to pay legal minimum rates.

At Big W, the wage increase was estimated to be worth about $40 million a year; at Domino's, more than $30 million. These were just some of the many similar-sized retail and fast-food chains that had to pay higher award wages from 2016 onwards.

The ACTU and Labor did their best to try to ignore a scandal that involved one of their biggest affiliates and cash cows. The ACTU secretary, Dave Oliver, said the Coles decision in the Fair Work Commission showed that the system was 'working', while also defending the SDA, despite it having done deals that had cut or removed penalty rates entirely. This came during a period when the unions and Labor were campaigning against cuts to penalty rates. It was profoundly discordant. Opposition leader Bill Shorten was more brusque about the union's failings, but was careful not to criticise it directly. It was the minor parties that did much to put the scandal on the agenda in Senate inquiries and in the media.

Cullinan is scathing about the lack of response from the Labor establishment, but not surprised. 'In reality, the silence or the complicity was basically saying these workers can be thrown under the bus, and they were for a long period of time, and they can be again in the future. They're part of the cannon fodder in ensuring that we have the power and influence that we want in our unions or in our ALP. It was unsurprising, really. I knew from my experience in the ALP the power they [the SDA] wield and the way the world works, and so I knew how that would impact. I guess I had thought that there might be an issue there from the Fair Work Commission, the Fair Work Ombudsman, or someone else with statutory responsibility to investigate and take action through the conduct of those who had completed the statutory declarations.'

There were only two ways for the problem to be dealt with, as far as Callinan was concerned: either the SDA would reform itself and change its behaviour, or an alternative union would have to be created. Doing nothing was not an option for him. The building of a new national union from scratch was unheard of in an era when membership was at historically low levels. In fact, an attempt by socialist activists to set up a rival to the SDA in the 2000s failed to gain traction, and fizzled out. However, in late 2016, Cullinan took the plunge. Freelancing to expose and take on the SDA while working at another union was becoming untenable, so, along with a group of volunteers, he created the Retail and Fast Food Workers Union (RAFFWU).

At the time, Cullinan told me: 'There's hundreds of millions of dollars being fleeced from these workers, and we are sick of it. The plan is for us to launch a strong, successful union led by retail and fast-food workers; they haven't had that for decades. We know that's a big task, and it will take time to build our union. But we have a sector of a million workers; half a million of them are subject to exploitative enterprise agreements.' Among its key figures were Michael Johnstone, a former SDA delegate at Woolworths Brunswick, who worked with Cullinan ahead of the new union's launch. Siobhan Kelly, the barrister in the Hart case, was its inaugural president.

Five years after its creation, the RAFFWU had about 3,000 members, still a fraction of the 200,000-plus that the SDA claimed to have. It was a significant achievement—it was bigger than the textile union was when it merged with the CFMEU in 2018—but it was still small. Its main impact is not due to its size, but to how it transformed wages and conditions in retail and fast food by agitating for and being active in killing off the old SDA deals. That's been worth billions of dollars to retail and fast-food workers. It has also moved into new areas of non-union retail, organising JB Hi-Fi workers on the subject of sexual harassment, and retail workers on rest breaks and toilet breaks. Even independent Newtown bookstore Better Read than Dead has been targeted: working conditions have been improved, including through the abolition of junior rates. 'These outcomes are within everyone's grasp if they have the capacity to take the action,' Cullinan said. The union has run member-led campaigns, as well as a series of legal cases where Cullinan's expertise has come to the fore. In one case, a Federal Court decision described the RAFFWU, through its representation of low-paid workers, as having served the 'national interest'.

Before 2021, the new union was growing at about 60 per cent a year, but the second year of the pandemic slowed its pace. 'We couldn't really foresee what would happen when we launched,' Cullinan said. With 3,000 members, it now has enough annual revenue to have a serious foothold, and is strong enough to survive with a growing team. However, it remains on the outer of the union movement—not affiliated to the ACTU or Victoria's Trades Hall Council.

If the union movement had the same membership density now as it did when Bob Hawke became prime minister in 1983, there'd be an extra four million union members in Australia. Instead, there are barely 1.5 million in total. Those members that remain tend to be older, and many of those most in need—in precarious work and casual employment—are rarely in unions. Australian Bureau of Statistics (ABS) figures show that the overwhelming majority of union members are in full-time work with paid leave. Decades of neo-liberalism and harsh anti-strike and workplace laws have stripped unions of power, making organising far more difficult. As have changes to the economy. Trade liberalisation since the 1980s and the rise of China have seen manufacturing shrink as a proportion of the economy. There's been relatively more work in the services and hospitality sectors, but with much lower levels of unionisation. The shape of work has changed, too, with more forms of temporary or precarious work, which unions have been unable to combat. The fear of outsourcing—both within Australia and offshore to the developing world—has induced passivity. Labour has been on the back foot for decades.

If you delve into the Bureau of Statistics data, the picture is even more alarming. In 2020, about 5 per cent of workers aged twenty-four and below were members of unions in their main job. For workers aged over fifty-five, the share was nearly a quarter of those workers. In 1990, union membership was about 40 per cent of the overall workforce; among young workers aged twenty-four or below, about 30 per cent were union members. About half of all older workers were unionised at that time. Now, as older workers retire over the next decade, it is likely that union density will continue to slide further. The ABS's data show that young workers are rarely exposed to unions; in some cases, they barely know they exist. The culture of joining, of working together, of going on strike is fading. It is what struck me when speaking to exploited chefs in the hospitality industry. This was a group of workers who wanted to work together and to improve their lives, but they did it outside the formal structure of Australian unionism.

We can see the significance of this shift in all sorts of ways. In recent election campaigns, anti-union attacks by the Coalition have failed to cut through. While once there were memories of when unions had power — back in the 1960s through to the 1980s — now claims that a big union such as the CFMMEU is going to destroy the joint, or that there are going to be job-destroying wage blow-outs, no longer work. The loss of members has been terrible for the unions, stripping them of extra resources and relevance. But the real significance lies in what it has meant for both non-union labour and inequality: in the sizable shift in the profit share from labour to capital since the mid-1970s. Without a strong union movement, workers have not been able to keep the same share of what they produce. (See Graph Eight.) The wealth of those on the *Financial Review*'s Rich List has ballooned.

Bottom 50% national income share, Australia, 1912–2021

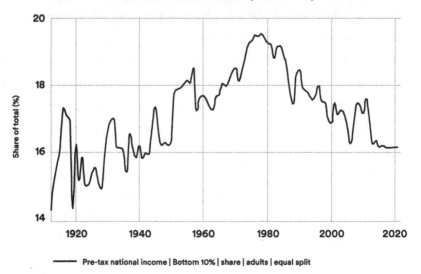

Pre-tax national income | Bottom 10% | share | adults | equal split

GRAPH EIGHT *Source: World Inequality Database*

Australia has become far wealthier since the liberalisation of the 1980s. But it is also significantly more unequal. It reversed the trend of the post-war years, when Australia and other rich countries simultaneously became more wealthy and more equal. The rise and fall of the union movement is an important part of that shift. Clearly, part of the solution is the need for a stronger labour movement, to be able to capture a greater share of the value that workers create through their work. The RAFFWU, which started from nothing, showed one way forward. As an activist union with just 3,000 members, it improved the lives of upwards of 500,000 workers through its creative approach.

There are many other unions that do fantastic work. The Australian Nursing and Midwifery Federation (ANMF), for example, has become the biggest and fastest-growing large union. In 2021, it had 313,648 members—more than 20 per cent of all union members in the country. A decade before, it had just 199,027 members. While the union movement has declined, the

ANMF has grown by 57 per cent. Over time, it has transformed what was a poorly paid female-dominated job into one with much better pay and conditions, and with respect for nurses. Through its campaigning, it has enshrined nurse-patient ratios in public hospitals that were eventually legislated. Other unions, including the CFMMEU in parts of commercial construction, have won some world-leading pay and conditions, while the Transport Workers' Union has done vital work in tackling gig work, particularly among delivery drivers. During the pandemic in NSW, both nurses and teachers went on strike, showing that industrial activism was not yet dead.

Yet the overall picture is not positive. The hole that the union movement is in is deep; the problems seem almost too large to be overcome. In the scheme of things, the 3,000-or-so members of the RAFFWU constitute only a tiny part of what needs to occur. There need to be a thousand RAFFWUs to rebuild worker power in Australia; in any case, its power, as Cullinan tells me, is still limited. Some of the gains it initially won have been wound back by shifting workers onto new classifications, from casual to part-time work, or shifting rosters, to dull the impact of the wage rises. The situation is still much better than it was, but it shows how fragile the gains were. In 2020, the Morrison government put forward a proposal to weaken the better-off-overall test for a period of two years—in effect, to allow companies to pay workers less than the minimum wage due to the impact of the pandemic. It would have been a return to a version of the old system that big business and the SDA had both utilised. In the end, the proposal was dumped, as it did not win minor-party support in the Senate.

Even with the election of a Labor government in 2022, the proposal lived on, with employer groups still pushing for changes to 'simplify' the better-off-overall test, claiming it would encourage more bargaining. No doubt, any changes they wanted would make it easier to pay some workers below the minimum-award wage.

The RAFFWU's success, no matter its small size, shows the importance of improving the lives of those in precarious or uncertain work through action, through rebuilding networks and restoring optimism. It is, by necessity, a slow, uneven process. The roots of organised labour's decline stretch back to the 1980s and 1990s, to the Prices and Incomes Accord—the collaboration between the union movement and Labor governments from 1983 to 1996. Government policy, in fits and starts, worked to curtail industrial organisation, reducing the real wages of workers. It was offset with not-insignificant trade-offs, including the social wage of universal healthcare and superannuation. There were many threads to it—and some countervailing measures—but, overall, it was a form of neo-liberalism with softer edges. Thatcher broke the mining union in the UK by using state power. Here, labour's power was reduced in exchange for things—some, admittedly, extremely significant ones, such as Medicare.

There has been much written about this period, from narratives of betrayal by some on the radical left, including Liz Ross detailing resistance from workers against the Accord changes, to Paul Kelly's magnum opus *The End of Certainty*, which argued that there was, in effect, no alternative to liberalisation and economic transformation. Kelly's was an epic tale of people who, in his view, fought against entrenched interests to transform Australia to enable it to enjoy a more prosperous future. Neither narrative tells a fuller story of the contradictions arising out of the period, of the costs and the benefits. To make sense of the Accord requires a complex interpretation of Australian history and political economy—beyond the narrower ambition of this book.

Yet it is important to recognise what the Accord did to the interests of workers. From 1983 to 1996, there was a significant reduction in worker power, a big shift in the profit share from labour to capital, and a steep rise in income and wealth inequality. As political economist Frank Stilwell noted in his review of the Accord, there was strong evidence that it led to a significant redistribution of income. 'The share of wages and salaries fell by approximately 10 per cent while the share of the gross operating surplus (including profits, rent and interest) rose correspondingly.' Was this a sell-out of workers? 'A more generous interpretation is that they expected those extra profits generated through the policies of wage restraint to flow through into productive investment, and thence into jobs,' Stilwell wrote. He described how the top-down process 'demobilised the labour movement', with rank-and-file unionists commonly feeling distant from it.

But, as Stillwell noted, it was impossible to re-run history without the Accord happening. He notes that the Accord of the early period, from 1983 to 1986, when there was a focus on regulation in the labour market, changed to an instrument that allowed wages to grow slower than inflation—effectively, to implement a wage cut. There were also cuts to tariffs, the privatisation of key government assets such as Qantas and the Commonwealth Bank, and the introduction of enterprise bargaining, which constrained the influence of a union to a workplace, rather than to an entire industry. This erected a platform from which the Howard government was able to implement—far more brutally—further neo-liberal workplace reforms and privatisations. Australia was re-made in this twenty-year period. The period saw a shifting of power from organised labour—which in the early 1980s had been able to win 20 per cent pay rises—to a situation where that influence has shrunk to such an extent that there has not been a major national strike in the decade or so since Qantas grounded its fleet in 2011. Even then, Qantas was the most active player in that dispute.

If you regard rising inequality as a serious matter, the problems from the Accord period onwards are still with us. Since the 1980s there has been no bounce-back—just a long-term trend of decline for unions. To be fair, there is a need to both recognise what the Accord wrought and to acknowledge that it was a response to the economic challenges of the 1970s: high inflation, unemployment, and slowing growth. Those challenges showed the limits of what a strong labour movement could do in an economy such as ours. Winning big wage rises was not enough if subsequent inflation meant little improvement in living standards. Without shifting to a significantly different type of economy, the decisions for the labour movement were hard. They tried to work within the system to reform it.

As Alison Pennington puts it, there were limits to what unions could have done, within the confines of the dominant ideas of labourism, to find a middle ground between capital and labour. 'Was protecting Australia's economy using the same tools amid growing globalisation an option? No. Did organised labour have the broader economic vision required to stem the powerful neo-liberal tide sweeping Anglophone economies? No. The sledgehammer didn't come down as hard on us compared to countries like New Zealand. We retained the awards system, for instance. But the playing field had shifted, and labour was losing power.'

She said the decisions made about where to apportion responsibility were choices. 'Holding workers' wages accountable primarily for inflation control was a policy choice—just like dismantling the manufacturing system over decades was a policy choice. Workers were told their pay was too high, and protections for manufacturing the reason why growth was slowing, rather than, say, businesses deciding their profit rates weren't high enough to justify re-investment.

'With globalisation, you've got an exponential increase in the bargaining power of business. When they say, "We will piss off and take the factory to Indonesia," they have the power to, because our own free-trade and deregulatory policies helped them to.'

United Workers Union leader Tim Kennedy regards the Accord period as one reflecting long-term shifts in power. The post-war years, he told me, were ones of 'accommodation' by capital, as it was 'on its knees'. That shifted from the 1980s, in particular, when the right embraced free-market intellectuals such as Milton Friedman and Friedrich Hayek. As Kennedy put it, that thinking influenced the business schools and a generation of executives and leaders. This has had a profound impact on all aspects of the country. That is why it is worth discussing how we got here, to work out where to go next.

Liz Humphrys, in her recent book, *How Labour Built Neo-Liberalism*, described the labour movement's contradictory role in Australia's transformation. In a poignant passage, she described the 'demobilisation' of workers through a decision of the Australian Manufacturing Workers' Union (AMWU) to close local suburban branches in 1988. The union had been communist-run, and had seen its role historically as being to educate its members, to build solidarity and class consciousness. One of its most significant leaders, Laurie Carmichael, a communist, had endorsed the Accord. He'd originally seen it as a 'transitional program for socialism'. However, the direction of the Hawke and later Keating governments dashed those hopes. By the late 1980s, as the AMWU did away with its local branches, the Coburg branch condemned 'the abrupt closure of the union residential branches without proper notice' or the provision of another structure to replace it. The final entry of the minutes book noted: 'Last and final meeting of the AMWU Coburg Branch 321 closed at 9:35 pm. Good luck and best wishes to all the loyal members who have attended the branch meetings over the years it has been in existence.'

Rebuilding those formal and informal links and networks, and unionism itself, may be, as Tim Kennedy told me, a 'two-generation' job. Of the 5 per cent of workers aged twenty-four and below who were members of unions in 2020, it is likely that a decent percentage had been signed up or encouraged by their boss to join the SDA. If history is any guide, it may be an inauspicious experience of unionism for them — if they register it much at all. As Cullinan put it, 'If workers can participate in direct action and get outcomes, they are transformed. They see the world in a different way.'

Chapter Seven

The golden arches

Wherever it has expanded, multinational McDonald's has brought a few things with it: Big Macs; cheap, predictable food; and a deep and abiding hostility to unions. Even for a US company, its antipathy to organised labour has been infamous. While becoming one of the most recognisable emblems of American capitalism, it has fought for decades to keep unions out of its stores. To keep wages low and unions out, it has used a variety of tactics. According to investigative reporting from *Motherboard*, activists pushing for a US$15 minimum wage at its American stores in recent years were treated as a security threat and spied on. An intelligence unit in Chicago and London used data-collection software, and monitored its workers to explore links between them and the campaign organisers.

The successful 'Fight for $15' campaign had sprung from McDonald's workers in New York City in 2012, who were demanding an end to poverty-level wages and the right to form a union without retaliation. It spread to become a national campaign across low-paid industries. Through it all, McDonald's refused to bargain with unions or to allow a union presence in its stores. It uses its franchising arrangements—much like 7-Eleven did in Australia—to draw a distinction between the conduct of its stores and of head office. It said the protesting workers in franchise stores weren't even its employees.

It has fought similar battles around the world. In the UK, it told McDonald's workers that they were 'totally free to join a union' if they wished to do so. This, it noted, was in accordance with 'UK and EU employment regulations which we follow to the letter. However, we don't currently work with any specific trade union because we have a number of internal methods that we use to speak to our employees all the time.' It was the classic language of major US corporations: *Of course you have a choice to join a union, but we'd much rather talk to you directly rather than to a third party.* In Australia, the approach has been different again: rather than fighting unions and trying to keep them out, McDonald's has allowed unions into its stores and even helped them sign up members. Yet this was not due to the local management's enlightened pro-worker attitudes. It turned out that McDonald's was able to get more from working with the SDA than from fighting to keep them out.

In 2016, as our investigation into the SDA's deals with big business gathered steam, we were particularly keen to focus on its dealings with McDonald's. It was Australia's second-largest employer, had tens of thousands of young people on its books, and appeared to have influential links to politicians in Canberra. Why was this famously anti-union company happy to work so closely with the SDA? Much of the answer to this question came in May 2016, when Nick Toscano, my colleague at *The Age*, was leaked an entire roster, along with hundreds of payslips, from a Sydney store. From that, we started to work on making sense of the hours that employees worked, how they were paid, and the scale of the underpayments. We brought in Josh Cullinan to help, and went over the calculations again and again to make sure they were correct. It soon emerged that the scale of the wage theft was shocking, far in excess of what had occurred at Coles or Woolworths. It was a significant story about a major company. McDonald's had become part of many people's lives through it having provided their first job, and was part of the fabric of suburban Australian life.

Within weeks of being leaked the rosters, we were ready to publish the results of our analysis. Our editors backed it heavily, and the article took out the entire front page of *The Age*, with a giant McDonald's logo and headline titled 'McExploited'. (See image on next page.) There was a brilliant cartoon from the late Ron Tandberg to accompany the piece. The reporting revealed that McDonald's was underpaying its Australian workers many tens of millions of dollars a year, and up to one-third less than they should have been paid under the minimum rates of the award. Our findings showed that 63 per cent of workers at the Sydney outlet were being paid below minimum rates, including young workers on as little as $10.08 an hour. The pay details of the 170 non-managerial staff showed that the worst-off employees almost always worked some weekend or night shifts. Combined, the underpaid workers at the store were $107,000 a year worse off than they should have been. 'The analysis shows beyond doubt that two in three workers are worse off,' Cullinan said at the time. 'It doesn't matter if they are young or old, if they are casual or non-casual. They are all worse off.'

$2.50
Friday
May 20, 2016
Published in
Melbourne since 1854
theage.com.au

THE AGE

— INDEPENDENT. ALWAYS. —

McExploited

REVEALED How one of Australia's biggest unions and McDonald's cut a deal to kill off penalty rates and pay the fast-food giant's employees wages way below the award.
PAGES 4-5

Macca's workers underpaid by millions

**Ben Schneiders
Nick Toscano
Royce Millar**

Burger giant McDonald's is underpaying its Australian workers tens of millions of dollars a year under a cosy deal struck with Labor's largest union affiliate that excludes weekend penalty rates.

A Fairfax Media investigation has found the Shop, Distributive and Allied Employees Association (SDA) negotiated a 2013 agreement under which some McDon-

ald's employees are paid nearly one-third less than the award - the minimum pay and conditions safety net.

Nationwide, workers at McDonald's - Australia's second largest employer - appear to be out of pocket by at least $60 million a year. Those affected include young workers who earn as little as $10.08 an hour.

The findings are based on hundreds of payslips, obtained by Fairfax Media, and the leaking of an entire store's roster that shows

68 per cent of workers at a large Sydney outlet are paid less than the award.

Brigid Forrester until recently worked up to four shifts a week at a McDonald's store in Perth, including Sunday evenings from 4pm to 10pm. She did not get penalty rates. "The weekends were tiring, terrible shifts to work," she said. "I would always joke with people about how bad our pay was, but I was struggling to pay rent, and I have to pay for petrol and for parking at university."

Substandard deals done by the employer-friendly union may be responsible for up to half-a-million workers in the wider fast food and retail sectors losing hundreds of millions of dollars a year.

The union is separately locked in a similar controversy surrounding its deal with Coles - the nation's third largest employer. The supermarket chain has since admitted tens of thousands of its casual workers have been underpaid.

The union's agreement with the country's biggest employer, Wool-

worths, is almost identical to the Coles deal.

News of the underpayments comes at an uncomfortable time for Opposition Leader Bill Shorten, who has made the defence of penalty rates a key part of his election campaign, saying this week "only a Labor government can be trusted to protect our penalty rates system".

SDA insiders have expressed concerns to Fairfax Media about a

∎ Continued Page 4

NEWS, Page 2
**Superbugs
among us**
CRE found in a
Victorian nursing home

WORLD
**EgyptAir jet
vanishes**
A distress call, and
then nothing

COMMENT
**Merely a
statement of fact**
Peter Dutton did nothing more than tell
the truth, writes **Malcolm Turnbull**

Weather
Today Partly cloudy   11 - 18
Tomorrow Partly cloudy   9 - 20
Sunday Mostly sunny   12 - 20
Details   Page 32

PRUSKA
**FAST DEBT
COLLECTION
NO RECOVERY
NO CHARGE**

Odd Spot
Almost 100 pupils at the Ersa Pereta Flores School in Tarapoto, Peru, are being described as being in the grip of a mass case of demonic possession. Experts are struggling to explain the phenomenon at the school, reportedly built on a Mafia graveyard.

BusinessDay
**Airbnb sued for
ignoring racism**
Page 24

McDonald's workplace agreement with the SDA included no weekend penalty rates, and restricted late-night rates to a mere 10 per cent loading from 1.00 am to 5.00 am. If workers had been paid fast-food award rates, they would have received penalty rates of 25 per cent on Saturday and 50 per cent on Sunday (with 75 per cent for casuals), as well as higher night-shift loadings from 9.00 pm to 5.00 am. Instead, in exchange for their loss of penalty rates, workers were being paid a few cents an hour extra.

It was an extraordinarily good deal for the multinational, while the trade-off for the SDA appeared to be the help it received in signing up members and getting a foothold in a notoriously anti-union company. This boosted its membership numbers and its overall influence in the ALP. The big losers were the low-paid staff across McDonald's, who were deprived of tens—potentially hundreds—of millions of dollars that they were entitled to. McDonald's response was unconvincing: a spokesman said it was 'wrong' to say staff were underpaid, as the union deal provided higher base pay rates across the entire week, 'as opposed to penalty rates that only apply to limited timeframes. We are a twenty-four-hour, seven-day-a-week business, and our employees tell us they love the flexible working hours we provide.'

That company response did not address, at all, the substance of the reporting or analysis, gliding over the stark fact that its deal had left tens of thousands of workers underpaid. The evidence was conclusive: the vast majority of workers at McDonald's would have been better off if they had kept their penalty rates. The reporting again highlighted how deep the problems were with the Fair Work Commission's processes. The commission was entrusted with ensuring that enterprise agreements left workers better off, but it had repeatedly failed to do so. In response to us, Gerard Dwyer, from the SDA, trotted out the true-but-irrelevant line that McDonald's workers were some of the 'best paid fast-food workers in the world'. Australia's relatively high minimum wages meant that you could say this about all workers, in whatever sector of the economy. These McDonald's workers should have been paid considerably more.

On the day of publication, there was a significant response from readers and industry players, and much follow-up reporting across national media. Ironically, this had the unintended effect of blunting the Labor opposition's attacks on cuts to penalty rates elsewhere, and highlighted the duplicity of its biggest affiliate, the SDA, in conspiring to cut basic conditions. The closeness between McDonald's and the SDA was reflected in some of the responses. Straight after publication, McDonald's Australia's chief executive, Andrew Gregory, wrote to franchisees, in a memo that was leaked to us soon after, telling them that the 'last thing' McDonald's wanted was to 'get into a public debate' about enterprise agreements. 'What we are working to do is broaden the focus of this story, to make it more about the issue of industrial relations and less about McDonald's.' Gregory said that McDonald's was in continuing, 'direct' discussions with government ministers, and with 'both sides of politics', about its stance on industrial matters. McDonald's was relying on its 'partners', including the Australian Industry Group and the union, to make its case in the pay-and-penalties debate. 'The SDA will continue to clarify the facts on our behalf,' he wrote.

It was an incredible statement. Here, one of the world's most aggressively anti-union companies was using a local trade union to justify its workers being paid below the minimum wage in that country. And the SDA, naturally, went along with it. For McDonald's, the conduct made immense commercial sense: the arrangements had been too lucrative to resist, so there had been no point in clinging to its anti-union antipathy.

On the other hand, if the SDA had been a traditional trade union aiming to improve its members' wages and conditions, the deal would have made no sense, and indeed would have been anathema to it. Yet this was the reality of some unionism in Australia in the early twenty-first century. Some unions worked with employers as part of broader political projects, and in the process were prepared to undermine the wages of their members. While much has been done to the union movement in the course of forty years of neo-liberalism — such as harsh anti-strike laws and restrictions on organising — this was a spectacular own goal. In the case of McDonald's, these exploitative arrangements were made at the expense of a group of young workers who were often having their first experience at employment and of unions. It was demoralising, to say the least.

One of the workers we interviewed, Stacey Clohesy, experienced all this first-hand. At the age of fifteen, she was paid $8 an hour to clean, take orders, and pack food at a McDonald's in Melbourne's working-class west. Her two elder brothers had worked there, too. 'The pay wasn't great,' she recalls. 'But it was my first job, so I was excited to get money.' In truth, Clohesy was paid less than the legal award rate. She got no penalty-rate pay, and took home just $147 for an eighteen-hour week.

Then, just a few weeks after starting work, she received a formal warning. After recovering from an injury, she'd been keen to play a game of football. Anyone wanting a day off at McDonald's has to arrange their own replacement. She did that, with her supervisor's knowledge, but, as her replacement was older, the shift was going to cost her employer an extra $20 or so. This was grounds for a written warning—one she had to sign, admitting her 'error'. 'Then they changed me to casual and didn't give me a shift for five weeks,' she told me.

She quit her job at McDonald's in Laverton after four months. She left to maintain her pride, her dad Colin said, after she received her written warning and was demoted to casual employment. McDonald's didn't even refund the $50 she'd spent on her uniform, despite this being in its legal agreement with the SDA. 'We don't have a lot of money, obviously,' said Colin Clohesy, speaking to me from the living room of his modest home. 'We live in a lower-working-class area; we struggle to make ends meet. But you can't do this to us for $8 an hour and expect us to hang in there.'

It would be easy to dismiss what happened to Stacey Clohesy as part of the natural experience of young people entering the workforce. So what if, in your first job, you are treated badly? Isn't this just part of a tough-love initiation into the real world? As this book has described, the real world is full of unfairness and exploitation. McDonald's itself leans into that narrative about its importance in the evolution of people's lives, of giving people a start. And it's true that, at one level, it is deeply embedded in Australian life. In 2019, it even boasted that since opening here in

1971, it had hired more than 5 per cent of the current population, or 1.3 million people. 'At Macca's, we're so proud to be able to offer so many young Australians what is often their first job. We take that responsibility very seriously and believe it is our privilege to provide them with the foundations to build skills for life, setting them up for future success,' Jennifer St Ledger, the company's chief people officer, said.

Cutting through the public relations spin of 'personal growth' and 'training opportunities', it's apparent that McDonald's has set itself up in Australia to take particular advantage of young people such as Stacey Clohesy. Australia's system of junior wages creates incentives for companies to hire young workers and to churn through them with rapidity. In the fast-food award, fifteen-year-olds are paid just 40 per cent of the adult rate. In 2021, that equated to as little as $8.93 an hour; for someone aged over twenty-one, the pay for the same work was $22.33 an hour. In much of the rich world, junior rates of pay are set at a much higher rate as a percentage of adult pay. Only the Netherlands has a lower junior pay scale: it is set at as little as 30 per cent of an adult wage, according to research for the International Labour Organisation. In some countries, such as Spain and Canada, there is no difference between a youth and adult wage, while in France it's set at 80 per cent of the adult rate.

For multinational fast-food employers in Australia, where there are relatively high adult minimum wages, the incentive to hire young workers is significant. To be able to pay young workers $8 to $9 an hour, lawfully, means that the make-up of a McDonald's workforce is very different here from in similar countries. Company filings with the Fair Work Commission put the number of McDonald's workers here under the age of twenty-one at about 80 per cent of its workforce. In the UK, 60 per cent are under twenty-one, while in France fewer than 2 per cent are under eighteen. In the US, fast-food workers at limited-service restaurants—not just at McDonald's—skew older, with 83 per cent aged eighteen and above.

The leaked data from one of its Sydney stores in 2016 provided Nick Toscano and me with further insight into McDonald's practices here. My analysis showed that 81 per cent of the workforce were on junior rates, and that one in six workers were fifteen years old. They were paid the lowest rate allowed at the time: $10.08 an hour as a casual, compared to the $25.70-an-hour rate for an adult. The average age of the workforce was eighteen, and there was not a single worker aged over thirty.

McDonald's was able to game the system further. On top of those dismal youth wages, McDonald's was paying less than it should have, as it had been able to trade away nearly all penalty and weekend rates under its deal with the SDA. The McDonald's business in Australia makes healthy profits: in excess of $300 million most years, after sending about half a billion dollars in service fees offshore each year. In 2015, when its deal with the SDA was still in existence, it made a profit of $572 million in Australia. McDonald's profits have slid in recent years, although working out the role of changes in labour costs is difficult, as it does not report the costs for franchisee-run stores, which are the bulk of its network. The shifting of money offshore is extensive, too, further muddying the true state of its profitability. Yet it is clear that McDonald's has skilfully used Australia's labour laws to suppress wages as much as possible. Its ability to pay young workers so little, along with its dealings with the SDA, has reaped it hundreds of millions of dollars in extra profit over the years. The whole system was tilted in its favour.

And, as one McDonald's franchisee admitted to the Fair Work Commission in 2018, the turning over of staff as they got older—as their wages lifted, increasing the labour costs—was standard practice. The so-called learn-and-churn model allowed it to keep costs down and profits higher. McDonald's denied this was a widespread practice, in the face of evidence to the contrary. Former fast-food worker Max Beech told the ABC he began working at a McDonald's store in Queensland when he was sixteen, and later moved to a Brisbane store when he was eighteen. Getting rid of older workers was an 'unspoken rule' between managers, he said. 'A lot of the time, they talked about how they were trying to get rid of certain people for this reason or that reason—a big one was when people were getting too old. So people turning eighteen or nineteen, they'd start to talk about phasing them out ... And that was a common thing.' Josh Cullinan told the ABC: 'The system that's used at McDonald's is exploitative, and it should stop. Not one of them is told, "When you get this job with us, when you blow out the candles on your next birthday cake, your hours are going to be cut."'

No doubt, many young people get something positive out of working at McDonald's—their first income, an experience of the wider world away from family and friends. Yet that's not the reason companies employ so many young workers in Australia. If youth wages were higher, as they are in many other rich countries, McDonald's would undoubtedly hire fewer young people. Yet McDonald's speaks of this formative working experience as though it were an indubitably good thing, whereas it has also exposed young people to a type of unionism that leaves them underpaid and basically unrepresented.

Naturally, many people would be keen to get out of the fast-food industry as fast as they could. But the mistreatment, the poor pay, the petty punishments, and the constant churn creates an exploitation machine, and prevents the building of skills. It doesn't have to be so. Nursing is a great example of unpaid or low-paid labour—once seen as the natural work of women—but it has been turned into better-paid work and professionalised. There are many jobs formerly seen as 'low-skilled' that have been transformed into good jobs through workers' collective actions.

Those who do best financially out of the status quo are McDonald's shareholders and executives. While some workers go on to become managers, most are churned through low-paid jobs. 'The implementation of very low youth rates generates incentives to [employ] low-productive young labour, rather than improve efficiency,' Professor Damian Grimshaw wrote in a paper for the International Labour Organisation. 'As young employees age, employers face a significant annual increase in labour costs and may be tempted, or pressured, depending on the context of labour and product market conditions, to substitute them with even younger workers.' That's been the experience in Australia, as the Fair Work Commission heard, and as the company's own employment demographics show.

McDonald's has been a company that's long had influence in Canberra. As the pay scandal involving big business and the SDA rolled onwards from 2015 through to 2017, those political links became more important. The issue itself seemed to throw the major parties off their regular behaviour. Typically, a pay scandal involving major employers would be easy fodder for Labor, which would champion the rights of low-paid workers and union members. Not this time. The involvement of the SDA—which, as we've seen, sponsored up to one-sixth of the federal caucus during this period—meant that Labor tried as best they could to avoid talking about it.

Adding to the complications was Labor's campaign against separate cuts to penalty rates in retail and fast food already made by the Fair Work Commission decision. With the SDA having already traded off these penalties—often, for next to nothing—the core of their argument was undermined. The

ACTU defended the SDA, typically by trotting out the 'best-paid fast-food workers in the world' argument, but with no great enthusiasm. Australia's biggest union, the Australian Nursing and Midwifery Federation—which is not affiliated to the ALP—was one of the few to break ranks and to condemn the SDA deals as 'reprehensible', noting 'sadly' that the union and employers had cooperated on deals that had left 'hundreds of thousands of low-paid employees' underpaid.

The Coalition moved between using the wage scandal as a stick to beat Labor with to, in the end, not doing anything about the underlying problem. Many of the companies involved were politically influential, with deep connections to prominent director networks. Coles, at the time, was owned by Wesfarmers, the conglomerate that had on its board corporate bluebloods such as Richard Goyder, Michael Chaney, and Business Council of Australia (BCA) chief executive Jennifer Westacott. Rather than responding to the Coles decision by rectifying a wrong and paying everyone the minimum award wage, Westacott lobbied politicians for the better-off-overall test—the test that requires no worker to be paid less than the award—to be weakened. In interviews, including on the ABC's *7.30* program, Westacott spoke out against the test as the representative of the BCA. But she was also a Wesfarmers director, which owned several businesses—including Bunnings, Target, Kmart, and, of course, Coles—that all had agreements with the SDA. Wesfarmers was on the hook for hundreds of millions of dollars in extra wages a year.

Much of the championing of the 250,000 retail and fast-food underpaid workers was done by the Greens, and later by the South Australia–based Nick Xenophon Team (NXT). At one stage, two Senate inquiries in August 2017 were concurrently looking at the SDA deals. Nearly all the heavy work in the hearings was done by these smaller parties. Xenophon was a force of nature who loved both receiving publicity and poking powerful interests in the eye. He took on this task with relish. Greens senator Lee Rhiannon, deputising for Adam Bandt in the upper house inquiry, was a persistent and dedicated questioner.

The Senate inquiries were able to call up executives from all the major fast-food and retail employers: Woolworths, Coles, KFC, and McDonald's. The inquiries also heard evidence from workers from companies that included Coles, Woolworth, and Myer. One Coles worker, David Suter, said he had been losing between $1,500 to $2,100 a year from the SDA agreement: 'Every hour and every shift I work attracts reduced penalty rates when compared to the award. I'm not looking for a handout. I want a fair day's wage for a fair day's work.'

When McDonald's was called up, Rhiannon confronted it with examples of an adult worker more than $4,000 a year worse off when compared to the award, and of a seventeen-year-old underpaid by nearly $2,000. McDonald's stuck rigidly to its line. There was no underpayment, it said, as the Fair Work Commission had legally approved the agreement. It refused to engage in specifics. McDonald's senior vice-president, Craig Cawood, was pressed by Rhiannon about who at the multinational knew about the underpayments. He admitted that McDonald's had not conducted a financial analysis to check if its workers were being paid less than the award overall., but said, 'I don't, in some ways, accept the premise of the question.'

KFC and Woolworths responded similarly, also claiming that they had not done a financial analysis of the SDA deals—a position that beggared belief. A senior Woolworths executive conceded that some of its workers might be being paid less than the minimum wage of the award. When she was asked during the inquiry, in response to our investigation, if more than 60 per cent of workers at a Melbourne Woolworths supermarket were paid below award rates, she said the company was unable to respond to that question.

KFC's chief people officer, Robert Phipps, was questioned about his company's agreement with the SDA, which allowed it to pay no weekend penalty rates and hourly rates that were only 9 per cent above the award. He would not answer directly. He said that KFC was in a 'positive place' with the arrangement. Answers to questions on notice regarding how much these workers were underpaid were never released publicly, with the inquiry accepting that they were 'commercial-in-confidence'.

All this pointed again to the interests of big business being put ahead of the public interest—in this case, the interests of low-paid workers. An inquiry chair, Labor's Gavin Marshall, expressed frustration at the lack of openness from the companies. But the response from the Labor members—which included several SDA-backed senators—was tepid. The Penalty Rates Committee's casting vote lay with Marshall and Labor, but the final report squibbed the issue, making no recommendations about the underpayment of retail and fast-food workers on SDA agreements. This was despite the fact that this subject was the very point of the inquiry, which had been initially moved by Xenophon.

The Coalition described Labor's 'hypocrisy' on penalty rates as 'breathtaking'. Employment minister Michaelia Cash said: 'The evidence presented to the Senate inquiry has been clear and overwhelming—under Labor's legislation, big unions and big business cut deals to slash penalty rates, without workers being informed about the deals being done.' Yet the Coalition did nothing, too: it opposed a change to the Fair Work Act later initiated by Adam Bandt to prevent SDA-style deals that would leave workers worse off. Labor, wedged on the issue, supported the Bandt amendments, which lost by just two votes in the House of Representatives. The political system had failed these 250,000 workers.

Despite this, the Senate inquiries produced some benefits. They provided forums in which big business and the SDA could be pressured over their dealings, and in which some answers could be demanded. It was a form of accountability, albeit in the end a frustrating one. The big employers were able to stonewall uncomfortable questions, and there appeared little follow-up to senators' demands for detail from executives about how much these deals had saved their employers. A Greens call for a royal commission into the scandal went nowhere. In the end, big business and the SDA, with their links to both major parties, acted together to frustrate calls for justice and reform. It revealed how stacked the political system was, as well as the failings of the SDA. It had failed badly in representing the interests of its members. Instead, it had operated as a phantom union, an entity to funnel numbers and money into its real project, pushing its political agenda and frustrating social reform.

The absurdity of the SDA's role was underscored after the Fair Work Commission finally, in 2019, returned McDonald's workers to the minimum wages outlined in the award—nearly three-and-a-half years after our investigation was published. The case had been brought by a McDonald's worker in his early twenties, Xzavier Kelly, who applied to terminate the old SDA agreement. Kelly, backed by Josh Cullinan and RAFFWU, calculated he had been underpaid $2,000 a year. 'To know I could have an extra $2,000 a year if I was just paid the award minimum, I could have used that. That's why I've done this, to apply to terminate the agreement. I think the crew should be paid what they legally should be.' Kelly's was another case of an ordinary worker taking on their employer and the SDA, and winning, as had Duncan

Hart, Penny Vickers, and Casey Salt. The commission's decision gave McDonald's workers full penalty rates for the first time, making a typical worker $1,300 a year better off, according to Cullinan.

Across more than 100,000 workers, the collective pay rise would be substantial, well in excess of $100 million a year. Over the previous decade, McDonald's workers had probably lost close to a billion dollars from its employer's deals with the SDA. They would never see any of that money, after the commission rejected a RAFFWU push for back-pay.

The response from McDonald's was swift. Soon after the decision was handed down, it cut off payroll deductions for SDA union dues. During the Senate inquiry, McDonald's said that about 15 per cent of workers in its company-owned stores were SDA members. There were no figures provided for its franchise stores. Now that it was no longer able to arrange a sweetheart deal with the SDA, it decided it would no longer make it so easy for the union to recruit members. In early 2021, McDonald's went further and said it would not negotiate with the union again; it would keep its workforce on the award, so wouldn't need to bargain with the union. This was a reversion to type for McDonald's, reflecting its anti-union stance elsewhere around the world. Later that year, the SDA sued McDonald's for denying workers rest breaks in its stores—an issue over which the RAFFWU had previously taken successful Federal Court action. McDonald's said that the SDA had been aware of the issue 'for many years' but had never raised a concern about it.

It was telling that the SDA was now pushing back against the multinational. It had never done so during the decades of wage theft, when the SDA was a trusted partner of McDonald's. It was only when the company cut off its lifeblood—payroll deductions, which were common in the pre-1990s era of closed-shop unionism—that it reacted. Cullinan expects other major companies to make similar decisions in the coming years. 'It doesn't take long for the employers to start wondering why they have a relationship with the SDA. Macca's is more ruthless in its approach, but some of the other employers, as they cycle through CEOs and as they cycle through HR departments and the rest, they will start making different decisions about how they support the SDA.'

What sense can we make of all this? While most unions do not operate in the way the SDA did at McDonald's, overall union membership is ageing, while wages growth is at record lows. This is a crisis for many Australian workers who are locked in precarious contracts or no contracts at all. Retail and fast-food workers have been doubly disempowered: their employer and union, in secret, worked together to deprive them of their basic rights and pay. Yet the millions of workers who experience insecurity at work—by the late 2010s, fewer than half of all employees were in a permanent full-time paid job with leave entitlements—are not storming the barricades. When the ACTU ran its 'Change the Rules' campaign ahead of the 2019 federal election, there were large rallies, and the union membership base was motivated. But, as the election results showed, workplace insecurity was not the major issue. This was in sharp contrast to the anti-WorkChoices campaign, 'Your Rights at Work', that helped defeat the Howard government in 2007.

There were many critiques of the 'Change the Rules' campaign, but another factor in its lack of traction might be that, after four decades of neo-liberalism, many people in casual or temporary work cannot imagine a different reality, or believe that a better future is possible. Or they care so little about their work—the precarity, the poor quality of many service jobs—that they're unwilling to invest in the struggle to change it. The public is now more sharply divided into winners and losers, whether on wages, housing, health care, wealth, education, or retirement incomes.

In the 2022 federal election campaign, the unions were largely silent. Workplace issues were not a major issue, and Labor suffered swings against it in some of its safe working-class seats to minor right-wing parties such as One Nation and the billionaire-backed United Australia Party. It was a worrying trend in what otherwise was a triumph for those advocating for progress on climate change, women's equality, and anti-corruption.

To reverse this growth in wealth and income inequality will require many changes—some small and some large. It will take time to rebuild worker power in Australia. Fundamental to any project of this type is to understand the underlying conditions of those in precarious work, and of why inequality is getting worse, so as not to make the same mistakes again. As Thomas Piketty notes, the evidence points to the golden era of post-war capitalism having been something of an aberration. A combination of high economic growth, the destruction of private wealth through war, and interventionist governments imposing high taxes on capital and income led to what was called in France '*Les Trente Glorieuses*', or the glorious thirty years, of 1945 to 1975. That post-war scenario will not likely be recreated; the conditions then were too unusual. Now, private wealth as a percentage of national income is back to levels last seen more than 100 years ago.

In the post-war period, the top income-tax rates were above 90 per cent in many wealthy countries, including in the US from 1944 to 1964. It's barely a third of that level now. In Australia, the top marginal tax rate was 75 per cent after the Second World War, and 60 per cent into the 1980s. It is now 45 per cent, and the trend—after changes by the Coalition government in the 2010s—is for flatter taxes, rather than greater progressive taxation. Ideally, government policy would be used aggressively to reduce inequality through far greater taxation of high incomes, wealth, and capital gains, and to then redistribute that income through a larger welfare state, and an expansion of universal health care, social housing, and public education.

Fundamental changes to the workplace relations system are required, including bargaining across sectors, to allow workers to build power from the ground up. The Fair Work system, implemented from 2009, carried over much of the neo-liberal baggage of the previous twenty years, including tight restrictions on what issues could be bargained over and on union organising rights. These include a twenty-four-hour notice period to enter a worksite, and limits on reasons for entry. Australia's laws around industrial action are among the most restrictive in the OECD, forcing workers and unions to navigate a labyrinth to undertake lawful strikes. Non-members, meanwhile, are able to free-ride and get benefits from union-negotiated agreements while not paying dues—a fundamental inequity.

These types of changes are vital to creating a fairer society, yet Australia's recent history has been dominated by neo-liberal policy. Major political change on inequality, for now, appears unlikely. Labor's loss at the 2019 federal election, when its campaign included proposals to reduce tax breaks on housing and franking credits, was another setback. Its successful 2022 election platform abandoned those proposals, and was modest on matters to do with inequality—most notably when it ended up supporting the Coalition's significant 'stage three' tax cuts for the highest income-earners.

But there are things that can be done outside the sphere of federal politics. What's needed, starting from somewhere, is a slow rebuilding of activism, of ambition, of a broader project than just refining workplace law (no matter how important that is).

The focus mustn't just be on pay. As the 1970s showed, there are limits to what can be done with wage increases alone, no matter how important they are. There's a need for workplace democracy, to renew and pick up issues left behind decades ago. Politics has been narrowed down to the act of voting in parliamentary elections. But, while most people work in a system that is more authoritarian than democratic, they have little to no say over the direction of their firm, of their tasks, or what contribution their work makes to their community and planet. The world of major corporations — of McDonald's, of Amazon, or, more locally, of Telstra, of Coles, and of ANZ Bank — is a relatively recent invention. It has evolved its own systems of governance, centred on the roles of directors and the rights of shareholders. Voting power, crudely, goes to those with the most shares and therefore wealth. It's fundamentally undemocratic, in a far more extreme way than the property franchise was in nineteenth-century parliaments.

There's also a need to experiment with all sorts of ideas, whatever their scale. Germany's stakeholder model of business governance includes having workers on boards. Piketty says that this system of 'Rhenish capitalism' has reduced the market value of German firms, but better reflects the variety of interests in a society. 'The point here is not to idealise this model of shared social ownership, which has its limits, but simply to note that it can be at least as efficient economically as Anglo-Saxon market capitalism or the "shareholder model" (in which all power lies in theory with shareholders).' The model has some merit — although it won't likely reduce inequality much on its own — but it can be an important step to a more democratic workplace and system.

There are other ways to change the model from below, to make firms democratically accountable and cooperatively owned. A small example is Cooperative Power, an energy-retailer set up by unions and civil society in Australia in 2020. Under the co-op's rules, it is not allowed to make a profit, and the use of any surpluses that are made is determined by its customer-members.

Surpluses can be reinvested back into the cooperative's business or directed to any cause by a members' vote. In 2021, Cooperative Power reinvested its surplus into a combination of a worker strike fund, into subsidised power for low-income members, into green power, into international climate causes, and back into the business itself. The cooperative is tiny, but the idea it has given expression to is a way forward. It could be extended quite easily, at first, to businesses that require limited capital to compete.

When a crisis strikes—as it did in the 2008 global financial crisis and the 2020 pandemic—governments can be pressured to do things that would have beforehand seemed impossible. Both the Rudd and Morrison governments used unprecedented amounts of stimulus—outside of wartime—in response to both the 2008 and 2020 crises. When Covid-19 threatened to devastate the economy in March 2020, Australia introduced a $90 billion JobKeeper scheme that had flaws but provided, in effect, a guaranteed basic income during the pandemic. When the next crisis hits, it is vital to be forearmed with ideas at the ready. Tackling inequality, along with climate change, should be the focus. A financing facility to nurture cooperatives—similar to the Gillard government's Clean Energy Finance Corporation—could help spur growth. It would allow them to compete and expand more quickly to challenge natural monopolies or oligopolies that service basic needs. In time, government procurement could be directed to—or favour—democratically constituted not-for-profit companies over ones that are not.

Some of these questions go to the heart of how we organise our society, economy, and working lives. Why shouldn't organisations be under democratic control, representing not just the interests of owners and shareholders? It is hard to imagine the system changing from above, with wealthy shareholders and institutions relinquishing their power. The interests are too strong and entrenched. So why not start from below, with mechanisms for workers, civil society, and customers to decide who runs a business, what it should do, where any surplus should go? That's a fuller view of a civic life, of politics, of participation, and of giving your work greater social meaning.

Chapter Eight

Slaving away

Sitting across from me in a suburban McDonald's in Melbourne's sprawling south-east, not far from Springvale, were a group of Malaysian farm workers. Near us were new-looking self-service machines, while the teenagers serving behind the counter looked harried. It was a winter night in mid-2018 as the farm workers and their families described what it was like being paid a handful of dollars an hour. It was incongruous hearing about workplace exploitation amid the bright lights and garish colours of the fast-food restaurant. McDonald's was a favourite meeting place for organisers from the then National Union of Workers (NUW), as the young Macca's staff never paid much attention to who was in the restaurant and how long they stayed. It was near impossible for the union to meet these workers at their workplaces, such was the hostility from farm owners and contractors.

That night was the occasion for one of numerous meetings I had through that period with farm workers from Indonesia, Cambodia, Myanmar, and the Pacific Islands, many of whom were here without legal visas. At times, the NUW took me along for house visits to meet workers living in overcrowded and often substandard accommodation. It was an eye-opening experience: hearing of and witnessing working and living conditions akin to those in a developing country, rather than the rich one we were in. In many of these meetings, the issue of pay was important — the wages were often scandalously low — but the stories I heard were about much more than wages.

The workers often spoke with great intensity about the fundamental disrespect they experienced — the bullying, the sexism, the racism — and about the extraordinary hours they worked, and of being yelled at to pick more broccoli, lettuce, or fruit. The abuse came from all directions — sometimes from the farmers, and sometimes from the supervisors (often drawn from the same cultural background as the workers), or from the dodgy contractors who had brought them to the farms. The south-east of Melbourne was a hot zone of union activity, with its peri-urban farms close to large populations. It was easier to access for the NUW than farms in the vastness of regional Australia. Often, the subject of visa status was danced around by the workers, and was communicated carefully. (The issue of their visa status meant that it became near impossible to identify the workers in many of the stories I wrote on the issue in *The Age*.) Some who had overstayed their holiday visas or other types of visa often then applied for temporary-protection visas so they could remain in the country.

These were some of the 'illegals', in the language of conservative Australian politicians — or, as Labor's shadow home affairs spokeswoman prior to the 2022 election, Kristina Kenneally, took to calling them, 'airplane people'. This was a dog whistle, trying to beat the Coalition at its own game of vilifying 'boat people'. Instead, Kenneally attacked the Coalition for allowing too many visa overstayers who had arrived by plane. Yet, whatever their visa status, these were the people picking the food that fed the country. By the mid-2010s, it was common for migrant workers on farms to be paid less than $10 an hour, with the pay nearly always based on piece rates. That rate was set by how much a worker picked, and was regularly set at levels too low to enable them to earn a decent wage. For decades, the wage theft in the industry had mostly occurred outside public view, with little to no union activity or regulatory action. The pressure to produce food as cheaply as possible—which came from the big supermarkets down—was being borne by these migrant workers.

Among the workers I met was Jeliah Jamon, who had been a computer engineer in Malaysia. 'When I came to Australia, I thought maybe I can use my career to do this, maybe a company will sponsor me,' she told me. 'I thought when I had that qualification, I could do something,' she said, her voice trailing off. 'Then off to the farm.' It was a reality for many workers from Malaysia, where the cost of living was high and the economy was suffering. Jamon had a friend who was a university lecturer in Malaysia but was now working in a factory. Jamon had worked at strawberry farms in Perth, Adelaide, and Melbourne earning $20 to $30 a day—or about $2.50 to $3.50 an hour. Eventually, Jamon was sacked after becoming pregnant.

Over the years, I met Mahani Tif several times; she'd become a union activist and public advocate for farm workers. Tif had arrived in Australia on a tourist visa in 2015, and got a job picking strawberries through a friend. The job came through a contractor, who also arranged transport. She earned $34.45 on her first day for packing nearly 40 kilograms of strawberries in crates, and had $10 deducted from her wages for transport. Her pay after deductions worked out at about $3 an hour. (The legal minimum wage for casual workers was well over $20 an hour at the time.) She would work seven days a week, for which she'd earn about

$175. Meanwhile, rent and bills in her share house cost her $100 a week. Later, at the end of the strawberry season, Tif worked on a cherry farm, and wasn't paid for several weeks' work. She then moved on to tomato-picking near Shepparton, where she could earn about $65 a day with $10 deducted for transport. That equated to about $7 to $8 an hour.

'We are always scared, and we cannot speak up,' she told me. Working conditions were poor, and the work dangerous, with injuries, from cutting fruit with a knife, common. 'When you work at a farm, there is no toilet, you have to go anywhere, in the bush.' Abuse, meanwhile, was commonplace. 'The contractor or the farmer used bad words, "Why are you fucking so slow?" We are always scared that when we complain that the pay is very low, when we speak like that, they will attack us and say, "Don't come to work tomorrow, just stay home."'

In mid-2015, the lid was lifted on what had been going on at farms for decades. An ABC *Four Corners* episode, titled 'Slaving Away', used hidden cameras to reveal the extreme exploitation of migrant labour, and to air allegations of abuse, sexual assault, and wage levels well below the minimum rate. It described working conditions as being akin to 'third world bondage', and exposed the 'dirty secrets' behind Australia's fresh food sold at major supermarkets. It quoted a union official saying that 'almost every fresh product that you pick up ... will have passed through the hands of workers who have been fundamentally exploited'.

'Slaving Away' described how labour-hire contractors preyed upon workers, who were subject to brutal working hours, degrading living conditions, and wage theft. 'There is slave labour in this country. It's something we need to get rid of; we need to address it, and we need to do it soon,' Coalition MP Keith Pitt told the program. 'I think you'd find that there's, ah, effectively a whole heap of crooks making an awful lot of money out of the exploitation of people who really don't know any different.'

Much of the material in 'Slaving Away' was drawn from the first large-scale attempt to organise workers in farms for forty years. The NUW had no legal right to do this organising work—under industrial demarcation rules, the Australian Workers' Union (AWU) was the union for farm workers—but it decided to do so anyway. An organiser with the NUW—before it later merged to form the United Workers Union—George Robertson, told me that the union had started organising farm workers around 2014. In the years before that, the NUW had focused on insecure and casual work in its 'Jobs You Can Count On' campaign. The point of its campaigns was to target insecure work across industries—not just at an individual workplace. The issue of insecure work was both damaging to workers, who were being pushed into precarity, but also to the union itself, which faced an existential threat. 'A lot of the union movement had found it really hard to organise casual insecure workers, even at their heartland sites,' Robertson said. 'You had situations where workers who were permanently employed were a much shrinking significant percentage of the workforce.' Every few years, the numbers of secure jobs would shrink further. It was a cycle that reduced the power of all workers at a site.

A pivotal dispute for the union had been at Baiada, in Laverton North, in Melbourne's west. The Dickensian working conditions at the chicken-processing plant had led to the decapitation of a Baiada worker, Sarel Singh, in 2010. I wrote about the thirteen-day picket line and strike in 2011, and images from inside the plant included uncovered raw chickens sitting atop plastic bags full of chickens, and cockroaches inside empty storage containers. There were also images of maggots and bits of raw chicken meat strewn about. Most of the workers, many of whom were of Vietnamese background, were either sub-contractors paid cash in hand or were temporary labour. The strike succeeded, and the chicken workers won restrictions on cash-in-hand labour and an agreement that temporary workers would be paid the same as permanent staff. A mass meeting of workers welcomed the win with cries of 'No more $10 [pay an hour]'. Robertson said the Baiada dispute—which occurred before he started at the union—had become a source of inspiration: 'It bust[ed] the myths that it's impossible to organise casual workers.'

The work at Baiada and the organising of poultry workers elsewhere led to a growing awareness at the NUW of what was occurring on farms. 'We had spent many years organising poultry workers. They had friends and family who were telling us about contractors, underpayment, horrible conditions in the horticulture industry, and so that was one of the inspirations in terms of getting started,' Robertson said. 'We had just started doing some farm-worker organising in a couple of areas—in the north of Adelaide and in the south-east of Melbourne, and going into Gippsland. The ABC wanted to do a piece on farm workers and the exploitation of farm workers. We ended up working really closely with the ABC to help them put that 'Slaving Away' episode together, which featured really heavily a lot of the organising work we'd done, and the workers themselves. That really launched the campaign to national significance.'

For decades, the Coalition had used the arrival of asylum seekers by boat to slam Labor as soft on the issue of border protection. Since 2001 and the *Tampa* incident—when the Howard government ordered troops to enter a cargo ship off the north-west coast of Australia with 433 asylum seekers on board—the issue had been particularly toxic for Labor. A month after *Tampa*, the September 11 attacks in the United States further inflamed anti-Muslim sentiment, conflating terrorism and the arrival of Muslim asylum seekers to Australia by boat. The mood of the time was captured by John Howard's formulation: 'We will decide who comes to this country and the circumstances in which they come.' The Howard government comfortably won a federal election later in 2001.

Kristina Kenneally's comments about 'airplane people' can be seen as an attempt to turn the 'soft-on-borders' attack back onto the Coalition government. It reflected a traditional Laborist concern about wanting to restrict exploited migrant labour, the idea being that this would boost or protect the wages of local workers. That position has a long — and often undistinguished — history in Australia's labour movement. From the start of the twentieth century, Labor supported various iterations of the White Australia policy, including the expulsion of thousands of Pacific Islanders who had worked in the Queensland sugarcane fields and had been brought to Australia sometimes as slaves. The policy was a feature of the country's politics for much of the twentieth century before falling into discredit. The Whitlam government's Racial Discrimination Act of 1975 signalled the legislative end of the practices.

Yet, despite the country being transformed since the Whitlam years by waves of migration from Asia, Latin America, and Africa, there remain particular public sensitivities about 'illegals' and 'queue jumpers' arriving here without a lawful visa. The beneficiaries of these attitudes have been and are unscrupulous employers. While temporary migrants are routinely exploited in sectors such as hospitality, the situation is worse for those with no legal right to be in Australia, as is the case of many farm workers.

Among the undocumented workers I met and interviewed over the 2010s was Yusuf (not his real name). Speaking through a translator, he told me that when arriving here he did not understand how the system worked. 'There was an agent that told me, "I can sort out your visa for you." I paid him $300. I got some sort of bridging visa, but it didn't allow me to work.' He said his life working on farms around Mildura and the surrounding districts depended on the contractor. 'Your life is pretty much controlled. The contractor just did not pay my wage [sometimes], and then there is no certainty when I can go to work.' Yusuf said he was supporting his family in Malaysia, including his mother and sisters, as his father had died. He had even slept in his car near Mildura, to help him send more money home.

Another worker I spoke to was also supporting her family back home. 'You don't want to go back to Malaysia. The economy is very bad, but everybody wants to take advantage of us, as we don't know anything,' she told me. 'The farmers, the contractors, the sub-contractors, the owner of the house, everybody.' She paid an agent $300 for a visa without work rights, and as an undocumented worker would earn $400 a week for a sixty-hour week picking oranges. Many undocumented workers, particularly on farms, are Malaysian. According to Department of Home Affairs figures, about one in six of all people here unlawfully in 2018 were Malaysian. They often arrived on a tourist visa, and whether they could work lawfully depended on when, or how, they applied for a bridging visa. Malaysians are not eligible to work here through the seasonal workers' program, which recruits temporary labour from the Pacific and Timor-Leste to work on Australia's farms.

Another undocumented worker I spoke to had laboured in Swan Hill picking stone fruit at $13 an hour for up to six days a week. He was told to sleep in a cool room. 'I was tricked by an agent, who promised me $8,000 a month, and work from 8.00 am to 3.00 pm, and a comfortable house. Before I came to Australia I was promised a working visa. The agent said, "Don't worry, I'll sort your visa out for you." When I arrived, I didn't understand the system or wasn't given information about my visa, and I was trapped in this situation where I didn't have work rights,' he said.

To survive, the workers live on their wits. One told me he was 'very careful who I speak to'. He'd pay a doctor $50 for a consultation and $80 for medication, as he had no access to Medicare. Working around Renmark, north-east of Adelaide, he estimated that about 90 per cent of farm workers in the area were undocumented. 'When I got here, I didn't really plan to stay here very long; it was more wanting to support my family because of the situation I was tricked into.' As George Robertson from the farm union said: 'We worked out pretty quickly that undocumented workers were the most exploited workers in the industry. But that, at the same time, there were regions where they made up the largest percentage of workers and where growers were structurally reliant on undocumented workers. There was this perverse situation where growers and undocumented workers were reliant on dodgy labour-hire contractors to employ those workers, and that anything you try to do to deal with that—whether through labour-hire licensing or through any other mechanism to try to raise standards for those workers, because they were operating completely outside the system—it wouldn't work.'

It was true, as Kenneally said, that these workers had been used by criminal networks and exploited. But what's the solution? Shutting the drawbridge hasn't worked—anywhere really. Credible estimates suggest that up to 100,000 people in Australia were working without a visa before the pandemic. If that estimate is correct, and if it has been maintained since, it would be close to 1 per cent of the workforce—a significant number of people. The rights of undocumented workers are more commonly seen as a problem in the United States or Europe, with their large, almost permanent, populations of such workers. It is estimated that about 4.4 per cent of the workforce in the US are undocumented, often from central and Latin America. This is often a major political issue in the US, with calls for the federal government to give an amnesty or a path to citizenship for non-citizens. Here, that debate is just starting.

What's most surprising about Australia's creation of a temporary-worker program and an underclass—whether here as undocumented labour or on short-term visas—is how open the exploitation is. In mid-2015, I received a tip-off to look into Chinese-language websites, including yeeyi.com, and some foreign-language Facebook pages. All were advertising thousands of jobs around the country. To read the advertisements I used Google Translate, which, while rough, revealed the pay, location, and type of work. They comprised a range of low-skilled and semi-skilled jobs on farms, nail salons, in construction, at factories, and in hospitality. Nearly all these jobs were being advertised at rates well below the minimum wage: it was a thriving market almost in plain sight, and routinely in breach of workplace laws.

As the laborious work of translating hundreds of job advertisements went on, I arranged to have three journalism students (and Chinese speakers) from Monash University help me. The students—Yanzhu Xu, Ivy Yuan, and Sunny Liu—were excellent researchers, and confirmed the translations and sometimes spoke to the people behind the advertisements. They found jobs being openly advertised as 'black' work, which signified an illegal job for people without work visas. The advertisers assumed that nobody much cared or was watching. In the end, we surveyed 1,071 job advertisements, largely aimed at prospective workers from China, Malaysia, Hong Kong, and Taiwan. It was common for jobs to be openly advertised at $10 to $13 an hour, significantly below Australia's legal minimum wage at the time of $21.61 for casual workers.

At the extreme end, our investigation uncovered workers paid as little as $4 an hour, and shady networks of middlemen who demanded extra payments from jobseekers to secure work. I spoke to one jobseeker, who did not want to be identified but said he had received death threats after a dispute with his middleman. These middlemen tended to be drawn from the same community as those they exploited. They'd take a cut from three sources: the workers themselves, the employers who hired the workers, and the owners of the cheap hotels that housed them. In Mildura, one middleman who hired out workers to local farmers also owned a caravan park, where he housed four workers in a tiny room. One Chinese-speaking middleman from Malaysia, who recruited farm workers, told one of the researchers enquiring about an advertised job that the work was black labour. When asked if he minded other jobseekers being told this, he said: 'It is no problem to admit it. I don't want the jobseekers [to] misunderstand the position.' Other advertised jobs demanded that workers pay $3.30 an hour from their wages, or several hundred dollars in up-front payments, to the middleman. In some cases, workers accused the advertisers and middlemen of promoting scams and fake jobs to steal from them. It was a giant swamp of rorts, all on websites with information that could be accessed easily.

Once we finished the research, we were able to report that 80 per cent of the advertised jobs we surveyed offered pay below the minimum wage. At the time, Australia had a temporary labour force of up to about 750,000 people, all with visas that limited their rights at work. Our analysis pointed to the high likelihood of hundreds of thousands of people being underpaid. There were, as discussed earlier, up to 100,000 undocumented workers here as well. By the time of the pandemic in early 2020, the program was even larger, and wage theft had become endemic, affecting up to one-tenth of the labour market. And the results of our survey were not a one-off. Research by Unions NSW in the following years found about 80 per cent of advertisements for jobs paying below the minimum wage. The organisation had expanded our research to look also at Korean- and Spanish-language websites. In November 2021, a Migrant Workers Centre survey of 700 temporary-visa holders found that 65 per cent had experienced wage theft, and one-quarter of them other forms of labour exploitation. It took workers, on average, 5.1 years to gain permanent residency, with one person waiting thirteen years. The report found a strong link between experiencing wage theft and not having a visa that offered a pathway to permanent residency. The centre called for more permanent visas and a cap on processing times.

The growth of an Australian guest-work program was never a formal policy or the result of a government announcement decision. Rather, a series of visa measures, successful lobbying from business, and the growth in the higher-education industry, in particular, helped facilitate it. It ran alongside the formal, long-standing, large permanent migration program that had transformed the country. From the post-war years onwards, Australia went from a nation of just 7 million people with a largely British and Irish background to one nearly four times as large seventy years later. That's reflected in about half of Australia's citizens now either having been born overseas or having at least one parent who was. Only Switzerland and Luxembourg boast a higher overseas-born ratio. Despite a history that includes the White Australia policy, the emergence of One Nation as a far-right party, and a political preoccupation, particularly from the Coalition, with refugees arriving by boats, few countries have managed immigration as well.

Yet the labour market today is very different from the one that greeted the many migrant workers who came here to live after World War II. Typically, newcomers then had permanent residency, and the legal and work rights that accompanied it. Today's temporary foreign workers are often here at the pleasure of their employers, with strict visa conditions tying them to their employer, or limiting the amount of hours they can work. Part of this shift has been due to an economic imperative — temporary visas have been used by businesses to fill 'skills shortages', but also to reduce the bargaining power of blue-collar unions and workers. The other economic factor has been the emergence of education as a new export industry, which has been pivotal to creating the temporary worker program. The higher-education industry expanded to accommodate increasingly students from poorer backgrounds, including from Nepal, India, and Colombia. Many had to work to support themselves. Others were students in name only, fodder for a flourishing new business in labour-trafficking, with sham training colleges used as a pathway to permanent residency. This led to the creation of a large and steady pool of international casual workers.

One worker on a visa we interviewed was Ryan Tseng, who, over four weeks, worked in a western Sydney meatworks for just $4 an hour. He was working in what was misrepresented as a training program – one that he finished unskilled, out of pocket, and disappointed by what had happened to him. Tseng had travelled here on a Working Holiday visa (subclass 417) in the hope of finding adventure, education, and decent pay. He paid $300 for what he believed would be four weeks of legitimate training in butchering—in particular, the skilled use of knives. Instead, he was put to work cleaning, packing meat, and lumping heavy machinery. He rarely got to hold a knife, much less learn how to use one. For fifty hours a week, and sometimes more, he was paid just $200.

Another Taiwanese worker we spoke to, Hanks Cheng, thirty-one, travelled to Melbourne on a working holiday visa in 2014, and through a Chinese-language website found a job in Geelong. Around that time, he was paid a casual rate of $15 an hour in cash to pick and pack oranges—with no tax, no super, no holidays, and no sick pay. The minimum legal rate at that time was $21.61. 'When we were in Taiwan, we call it "black labour," Cheng says. 'Always cash in hand, no tax, no super.'

In 1907, Justice Henry Higgins made a decision that has influenced the relationship between labour and capital in Australia ever since. The *Sunshine Harvester* decision set a minimum wage at a relatively high level — seven shillings a day. This was 27 per cent higher than the prevailing journeyman's wage, and was based on the need for him and his family to live in 'frugal comfort'. Skilled tradesmen received 10 shillings a day. The decision acknowledged a fundamental imbalance in the relationship between labour and capital. 'I cannot think that an employer and a workman contract on an equal footing, or make a "fair" agreement as to wages, when the workman submits to work for a low wage to avoid starvation or pauperism ... for himself and his family,' Justice Higgins wrote on 8 November 1907. 'Or that the agreement is "reasonable" if it does not carry a wage sufficient to ensure the workman food, shelter, clothing, frugal comfort, provision for evil days.'

The *Harvester* decision struck a balance between interests, but also set a minimum wage that was not determined solely by market forces — which has enraged conservative critics ever since. The decision did not occur in a vacuum. The previous decade had been marked by significant conflict — notably, the shearers' strikes of the 1890s — between business and workers. Police fired at strikers, and eight shearing sheds were burnt in one district alone in Queensland. That violence came after attempts by employers to cut the wages of workers in response to a recession. However, the armed conflict did not cascade as it did in the United States at the time, when there were dozens of fatal disputes.

In Australia, there was an accommodation of the interests of labour and capital. The *Harvester* decision was one of a series of measures that gave twentieth-century Australia its distinctive shape, with high tariffs, the White Australia policy (to keep out low-paid foreign workers), and the institutional adoption of a living wage to provide a relatively generous life for workers. It was an attempt to avoid the class stratification of old Europe. Yet the process was paradoxical: it was notably more egalitarian than in similar countries, but also based on racism through the White Australia policy.

Since the *Harvester* decision, Australia has maintained some of the world's highest minimum wages along with, to a certain extent, an idea of a living wage. Yet in the 1980s, as Australia's economy was hit by a downturn, and the old economic model fell apart, there was the assault on Higgins' legacy from the H.R. Nicholls Society, big business, a new class of economists, and much of the Liberal Party. H.R. Nicholls Society president Ray Evans once said that the *Harvester* decision was an exercise in economic vandalism by a 'mad' judge. In 1983, then opposition frontbencher John Howard said, 'The time has come when we have to turn Mr Justice Higgins on his head.' By the 2000s, WorkChoices was the vessel chosen by Howard, as prime minister, to do just that. The idea that there was a fundamental power imbalance between labour and capital was history. Yet the attempt failed. To a large extent, Howard lost government at the 2007 election over the issue of workers' rights.

Once WorkChoices was repealed by the incoming Labor government, its replacement, the 2009 Fair Work Act, can be seen as an attempt by the new government to hold the old *Harvester* ethos together, to reconstitute it—no matter how imperfectly—by injecting an idea of 'fairness' back into the system. Now, when deciding the minimum wage, the Fair Work Commission must consider the impact of its decisions on the competitiveness of the economy, and must also promote social inclusion through increased workforce participation and the relative living standards of the low-paid. The writing of these objectives into the Fair Work Act has echoes that go back all the way to the *Harvester* judgment and Justice Higgins. The Act requires the commission to set a minimum wage, not just based on market forces, but on broader social concerns (no matter how limited).

But the *Harvester* decision of 1907 reflected a long-gone industrial world made up largely of male (and white) full-time labour. Today, social change, the fissuring of permanent work, and Australia's guest-worker program mean that many people are not paid to work in 'frugal comfort'. They are obliged to do gig work, or a few hours of casual work a week, or can be moved from contract to contract with no security of tenure. They may or may not be in poverty, but either way that's not something that their employer has to account for. The fissuring is seen most graphically in Australia's horticulture sector, where cheap food comes at a cost. The beneficiaries of the system are producers and supermarkets, although smaller producers are often squeezed by the supermarket duopoly.

The shape of the farm sector is changing, too. Big capital is replacing older family farms, creating new distinctions. One of Australia's richest families, the Smorgons, was a big investor in Perfection Fresh, a major producer north of Adelaide. In 2015, the ABC's *Four Corners*' 'Slaving Away' report exposed worker underpayment and exploitation at the company, then known as D'Vine Ripe. Elsewhere, Costa Group, a horticulture producer listed on the stock exchange, has also been accused of underpayment. It made the transition from family-owned business to big business organically, yet the patterns of alleged exploitation are the same. After being challenged by the NUW, Costa's berry business—marketed under the Driscoll's brand—was forced to withdraw a workplace agreement that was much worse than the award, as it had cut penalty rates and had no cap on maximum weekly hours worked. Its berry business, meanwhile, had not negotiated an agreement with the union since the 1990s. And among smaller, poorly capitalised producers, conditions were often worse. Wage theft was routine.

On an industry-wide basis, it's hard to even attempt to justify wage theft within the horticulture industry as a way of employers compensating for a lack of profit, as the industry overall makes healthy surpluses. Bureau of Statistics data for agriculture—which includes horticulture—show that the sector made just under $10 billion in operating profit before tax in 2019–20, up by one-quarter over the previous decade. The data showed that two-thirds of agricultural businesses made a profit or broke even, with their pre-tax profit margins close to 13 per cent on average. Separate data from the Australian Taxation Office pointed to profit margins in the more narrowly defined fruit and tree-nut production sector at about 12 per cent, with wages representing a little over one-fifth of turnover. There were, of course, exceptions: some farming businesses were too small, and at the mercy of the supermarkets, which pushed them hard for lower prices. They struggled to survive and to pay legal minimum wage rates.

The UWU's George Robertson told me that the union's early organising efforts in the mid-2010s were able to change things. 'It was very crude. It was growers who had just become used to completely having their way with absolutely no accountability ... We tackled a lot of flat-rate cash underpayment in the early days. It was very, very common for employers, particularly focusing in the south-east of Melbourne and Gippsland down to the north of Adelaide ... those contractors were paying workers less than a minimum wage. Sometimes, usually significantly less. It was common in 2014 and 2015 for workers in the south-east of Melbourne to be paid between $12 and $14 an hour. It was common across all of the major farms.'

As the union's organising work started to gather pace, pay rates were lifted. Farmers started wanting praise for paying the legal minimum, Robertson said. 'The interesting thing is that a lot of times when we first started organising, growers wanted a pat on the back for employing people and paying them the award. I think there still is that perception in the industry now that the award has become the norm, that that's where it stops. That if we pay the award, that's it.' It was an important and telling shift in an industry that had been transformed in just a few years. Now the battle was not about how much farm workers would be underpaid by, but rather whether they should be paid anything above the minimum wage. Their pay was still low, set at or near the minimum award wage, but for these farm workers it was a significant advance in their living standards.

Chapter Nine

Fightback

When Tulia Roqara came to Australia in 2018 to pick tomatoes, she hoped to make enough money to set up a pastry shop back home in Vanuatu. While she was in Australia, her husband was labouring on a farm in New Zealand, and the couple's children were being looked after by Roqara's mother. It's not uncommon in the nations of the Pacific Islands for people to work overseas and send remittances home. I first met Roqara in May 2018 in a caravan park outside Shepparton, and she was direct and brave. The shabby caravan park was in the back blocks of rural Victoria, and I'd snuck in one Tuesday night with George Robertson to meet her and some other workers. There were dozens of Ni-Vans (as the ethnic groups from Vanuatu are known) living there, all having worked for the same local farmer for the previous five months. Roqara was one of a group of about fifty workers from Vanuatu who were paid as little as $8 an hour. After having hoped to save enough to set up a pastry shop, she was about to go home with next to no savings.

The workers had been paid piece rates, which was meant to encourage them to be more productive, benefitting both them and the farmer—a so-called win-win. The horticulture award stipulated that an average competent employee had to earn 15 per cent more than the minimum hourly rate for piece work, or more than $25 an hour if they were a casual employee. The Ni-Vans were employed by one of the country's biggest rural labour-hire firms, Brisbane-based Agri Labour Australia. It had told them that an average worker would earn at least $28 an hour for a thirty-hour week. Instead, their pay was significantly less, regularly only $8 to $14 an hour. They were also overworked, and for one stretch, over summer, laboured for fourteen days straight. Once their rent, visa fees, transport, and other costs were deducted, they were left with barely enough to go shopping for food.

Again, their grievances were not just about pay. Roqara, along with her co-workers, told me that they were exposed to dangerous working conditions, including inhaling an intense chemical stench after spraying at the farm. It was particularly strong as they knelt down to pick tomatoes. 'It was really hard to breathe it in, especially when we start picking. I got chest pains, and others [workers] got bleeding from the nose and the ears.' After they complained, they were told by an Agri Labour supervisor to keep working and to use Vaseline and cotton to stop the bleeding. The farm owner, Cesare Mercuri, disputed the claim, and said the problem may have been that they did not have enough water. But the workers were adamant. Mercuri also told me he had no choice but to pay piece rates. 'We can't pay hourly rate—we'd go broke in a couple of months.'

It's a common refrain from those employers who are prepared to talk about their side of Australia's wage-theft problem. And Mercuri was almost certainly telling the truth. Small and under-capitalised businesses often struggle to make a decent return, with their profits squeezed by big business. This is particularly true in the farm sector. Further up the supply chain, the big supermarkets operate under the logic of share market-listed capitalism, where maximising profit is the overriding concern. Miss your profit targets, and you'll be punished by investors; internally, senior executives are liable to lose their bonuses or even their jobs if the financial performance is poor enough. To them, the concerns of small Shepparton tomato farmers and Ni-Vans pickers is a distant—or non-existent—concern.

To keep the price of tomatoes low at the farm west of Shepparton, workers were threatened. Another Ni-Van worker, Kaspa Mwea, claimed that an agent from Vanuatu, on behalf of Agri Labour, told him and his colleagues that they would not be able to return to Australia if they joined the union. The workers were employed under the Seasonal Worker Programme, which is meant to provide the most stringent labour standards in the sector. Farms get access to a reliable pool of labour, and workers from the Pacific and Timor-Leste earn award wages far beyond what they could make at home. Well, that was the idea. Instead, there was wage theft, serious safety problems, and threats. It had echoes of the widespread mistreatment and enslavement of Pacific Island workers in nineteenth-century Australia, the so-called blackbirding that saw people kidnapped and enslaved to work on sugar plantations. And this mistreatment in the 2010s was at the reputable end of labour hire.

It was a similar tale in 2017 at Perfection Fresh's South Australian greenhouse operation—one of the biggest tomato-growing operations in the southern hemisphere. Seasonal workers, often from Vanuatu and also drawn from the Seasonal Worker Programme, told of being underpaid, of having substantial fees deducted from their pay, and of being threatened by their labour-hire employer. 'I was working five days a week, Monday to Friday, thirty-eight hours, and my payslip was around $800 a week. But with deductions, I am left with $500. We decided to join the union,' one worker said. These workers at Perfection Fresh were employed by MADEC, another significant rural labour-hire company, and the biggest user of the seasonal program. 'If you want to come back [to Australia], you have to leave the union,' another worker said he had been told. 'I want to come back. I was scared of his words. So were others, and some people resigned from the union that day.' MADEC's chief executive told *The Age* this was a 'misunderstanding'.

Perfection Fresh had overhauled its labour practices after featuring in the 'Slaving Away' episode, and had brought in MADEC. Here were two of the largest rural labour-hire providers in Australia, MADEC and Agri Labour, both at the reputable end of the industry, and both were accused of exploiting migrant labour. Union secretary Tim Kennedy said that the 'systemic exploitation' throughout the agriculture sector was the result of the price wars waged by major supermarkets. He said this was forcing farmers to squeeze labour-hire firms, who in turn recruited the cheapest possible labour. 'The system is broken.'

Yet, over time, the pressure exerted by the union worked. Through a combination of union organising, the leadership of worker activists, the use of the legal system, and public exposure, conditions improved. Within a year, MADEC significantly improved its observance of workers' rights, and fruit pickers were paid legal wages. Agri Labour eventually settled with Tulia Roqara and her colleagues, collectively paying them out hundreds of thousands of dollars. 'The most important thing, it's not all about the money. [It's] that we have the same rights Australians have,' Roqara told me.

As part of the settlement, the workers who brought the claim released a brief statement saying that they had taken legal action because they had been underpaid and threatened by an agent from Vanuatu. The Fair Work Ombudsman separately took action against Agri Labour. As part of an enforceable undertaking, the company was required to reimburse $50,823 to nineteen workers. The federal government's Department of Employment, Skills, Small and Family Business confirmed that Agri Labour had been suspended as an approved employer under the seasonal programme. The department spokeswoman said it made that decision because it took 'matters concerning breaches of laws and the correct payment of seasonal workers very seriously'.

For decades, it had been regarded as too hard to organise workers in horticulture—the sector with the most exploited workers in the country, many of them with no legal right to be in the country. Yet union activism worked. People started getting paid properly, and big labour-hire firms and farmers started to change their practices. None of this would have happened without union involvement, which had only started several years before. The activism and the industrial and public pressure had a cascading effect. There were public inquiries, legislation was introduced to combat the exploitation, and in 2017 the Turnbull government changed the Fair Work Act to lift tenfold the financial penalties for the most serious labour exploitation. Labour-hire licensing was introduced in Victoria and Queensland, and the Fair Work Ombudsman recovered more than $1 million for workers after they targeted the farm sector. The ombudsman's 'Harvest Trail' investigation—completed in 2018—found some foreign workers in conditions close to slavery.

The Ombudsman's Jennifer Crook said the investigation had been confronting. 'In some cases, the FWO encountered situations where a person is virtually bonded like a slave to a particular [labour-hire] provider, on the basis they have been told they won't have their visa extension signed unless they see out the season with them,' she said. 'We have had cases where [workers] are driven to their accommodation via ATMs and asked to provide money in advance for bond, transport, and accommodation costs. We saw backpackers being lured to regional centres by dodgy labour-hire operators, treating them poorly, bullying and sexually harassing them and ripping them off to the tune of hundreds—and sometimes thousands—of dollars per person.'

Some of the changes in the sector may have occurred without the union's organising—the ombudsman could have still made its inquiries, for example—but it is hard to imagine that the shift would have been this profound. The energy unleashed from the activism also transformed the political debate. In late 2018, the Victorian Farmers Federation (VFF) joined the union in calling for an amnesty for undocumented workers. Emma Germano, from the VFF, told me that the use of undocumented workers on Australia's farms was rampant and that significant change was needed. 'It's not a secret to anyone there is a black economy and there are a number of workers that are undocumented and living in the country.' She said the large-scale use of undocumented workers has been part of the system for 'many, many years, twenty years plus. Currently, the system rewards those doing the wrong thing.'

Germano admitted that she had used an Asian contractor to bring in foreign workers to work on her own South Gippsland farm. 'There were a few incidents that made it quite apparent some of the workers were undocumented.' She wanted to comply with the law, so she brought in legal backpackers to replace the undocumented workers. Overnight, productivity halved, as the backpackers were far inferior workers. It nearly sent her business broke. 'You are needing an industry to be compliant, and we need steps and transitions out,' she said of the move towards an amnesty. At the time, the federal Department of Home Affairs said it did not support an amnesty, as it 'would undermine the integrity of Australia's visa programs and would encourage non-compliance and further worker exploitation'.

By 2021, four National Party MPs, including Anne Webster, who holds the rural Victorian seat of Mallee, supported an amnesty. Webster said there were good growers in her seat doing the right thing. 'Then people down the road are paying people exploitative rates, both selling products to the market at the same rate, which is unfair and unreasonable,' she said. Webster argued that giving all undocumented migrants a path to a visa with work rights would level the playing field by giving them the opportunity to work at legitimate businesses paying lawful wages. Something that had been unthinkable only several years before—an amnesty for undocumented workers — was now winning support from a conservative rural political party.

There was more significant change to come. The AWU, which had the legal right to represent workers in the sector, brought a case to the Fair Work Commission to change the horticulture award in late 2020. The UWU—which represented the bulk of farm workers—later joined it and made its own submissions. The AWU-led claim sought to stop the worst of the exploitation and to ensure that workers were paid at least the casual award rate of about $25 an hour.

For decades, farmers had used piece rates as the main way to pay—and regularly underpay—workers. The piece rate was not, on paper, meant to be a vehicle for exploitation. Rather, it was designed to reward and encourage the most productive pickers and to pay the average worker more than the minimum wage. Yet this rarely occurred, and there was little oversight of the rorts. As the graphic examples of wage theft have shown, workers could be paid a fraction of the minimum wage, sometimes as little as $3 an hour. AWU national secretary Dan Walton said, while launching the case, that 'worker exploitation, worker abuse and even modern slavery is rife on Australian farms ... The farm employers' lobby is fond of claiming that fruit pickers on piecework arrangements make more than the minimum wage. If that's true, then they should have zero problem with supporting our amendment.'

In November 2021, the Fair Work Commission delivered its verdict: it found that the piece-rate system was 'not fit for purpose' and did not provide a fair safety net, that growers had set piece rates unilaterally, and that a 'substantial' proportion of workers earned less than the minimum wage. In reporting its decision, it said, 'The totality of the evidence presents a picture of significant underpayment of pieceworkers in the horticulture industry when compared to the minimum award hourly rate.' The commission stipulated that workers had to be paid at least the minimum award wage at all times.

The piece-rate system was as good as dead, as there was now little incentive to use it to cut wage costs. Growers, predictably, warned that the decision would have disastrous consequences, with Mark King, the chairman of Dried Fruits Australia, calling the decision 'shocking'. 'Where are we supposed to pluck those [more productive] workers from? ... Do you think the worker earning $25 an hour is going to keep working harder? No, he'll naturally slow down because there's no incentive for him.' Yet, of course, most of the economy works on that very basis, with no piece rates for most types of labour, and workers paid an hourly rate. The AWU's Dan Walton said that the Fair Work Commission decision would set a floor for workers. 'Now it will be easy for workers—even if they don't have good English-language skills or Australian connections—to understand if they're being ripped off. From now on, if you're making less than $25 an hour fruit-picking in Australia, your boss is breaking the law and stealing from you.'

It was a seismic win for the AWU, which had launched the case, won the legal claim, and skilfully exposed deplorable conditions on farms through the media and the workplace tribunal. It was a victory for a particular type of unionism. The union had few members working on farms, but it had used the industrial relations system and public relations effectively to improve conditions significantly. It was not the first time that piece rates had been in the spotlight. In 2009, the then Labor workplace relations minister, Julia Gillard, intervened with the Fair Work Commission to save piece rates and to ensure there was no flat minimum rate for workers. She'd been under pressure from growers to keep the piece-rate system under the new horticulture award. In those days, there was no real union activity, organising, or pressure in the sector, despite the AWU being an influential political player in Canberra. This time, in 2021, with a conservative government in power, the political conditions looked, on the surface, to be far less favourable for unions. Yet now there was an acknowledgement from elements of the governing National Party and industry groups that change was needed.

The big difference was union activism. The issue of worker exploitation on farms had also received significant media attention with investigations by the ABC and Fairfax in particular. As George Robertson from the UWU told me, it was years of slog. 'It is difficult to organise workers in a non-union industry. The hostility level and the fear factor necessitated that we organised a lot, and did a lot of organising away from the workplace.' Workers came to trust the union when they started to see results, he said. Similarly, growers knew they had to change. Robertson said that from 2014 onwards, wages started to improve — by as much as $10 an hour — in areas such as south-east Melbourne and the north of Adelaide. 'That's because growers knew that we were active. Even then, there was this interesting knock-on effect where there were those farms where we directly tackled underpayments and exploitation in a very public way, where workers spoke out publicly, where we had to take legal action against some growers and labour-hire companies,' he said. 'That really sent a message to the rest of the industry that they needed to clean up their act. Whether directly or indirectly, it had this flow-on effect to where workers, either through direct involvement or just as a result of them getting active in the union, significantly shifted the prevailing [pay] rate in the region.'

There was nothing particularly new or fresh about what the UWU's farm team did to transform the wages and conditions of the most exploited workers in the country. It was old-fashioned grunt work. 'It wasn't coming up with innovative schemes to magically make outsourcing of labour-hire workers go away,' Robertson said. 'It was, like, organise the workers really well through house visits and off-site organising, build relationships with community leaders at the workplace, and bring them together and take on the employer. That's what that model was. It was very simple, and that, I think, built confidence in the union that it's not impossible to organise migrant workers, and it's not impossible to organise insecure workers … There's been an obsession within the union movement of what's the latest trick? Or what's the latest new thing, the new model? I guess what we've tried to do is to take the most simplistic and basic organising approach possible.' And it worked.

There are echoes of this success throughout labour history. The *Harvester* decision came after years of social unrest and strikes, and the system accommodated such activism by creating a living wage. After tramways leader Clarrie O'Shea was jailed for contempt of court in 1969, a general strike paralysed Victoria. Soon after he was released, the penal powers—used to jail union leaders for not paying fines—were rendered obsolete. Activism can create change. The legal and industrial system shifting is often a manifestation of social and economic pressure, rather than the other way around.

However, while systemic changes can be imposed by courts or parliaments, they are vulnerable to being watered down or abandoned if they don't have a solid base in the affected industry or community. For years, the Transport Workers' Union ran a campaign around driver safety, and eventually succeeded in having the Gillard government establish an industry tribunal and binding pay rates for owner-drivers. It was a big win. But just as the tribunal's orders were to be implemented, a push-back from head contractors and middlemen (who hire the owner-drivers) led to those drivers revolting. The drivers drove to Canberra, and, as former ACTU assistant secretary Tim Lyons put it, demanded 'the right to be paid less and have fewer rights'. The Turnbull government swooped in and abolished the tribunal. That would have been much harder to do if the workers had been more unionised.

Much is out of the control of the labour movement. Institutions that favour the status quo are very powerful and influential, while capital has become much stronger, with one consequence being that we live in a society that is far more unequal than it was a generation ago. The fissuring of work into smaller and smaller tasks, and the explosion of jobs with little or no job security, have weakened the ability of unions to organise workers, and of workers to organise themselves. Much of the commercial media is owned by a handful of billionaires, and the coverage of unions in those media is often hostile. It has been forever difficult for unions and workers to get much favourable coverage.

Yet change can still occur. The RAFFWU, set up on a shoestring, but fuelled by injustice and the efforts of ordinary workers, led to billions of dollars in higher wages accruing to workers. It now has 3,000 members. The farm workers' union, starting from scratch, transformed working conditions among the most exploited workers in the country in a handful of years. It has more than 5,000 members, union secretary Tim Kennedy confirmed in early 2022. They're small examples, but they show that change is possible in even the most hostile environments. Or look at the Australian Nursing and Midwifery Federation, which became the strongest union in the country by transforming poorly paid female-dominated jobs. None of these outcomes was inevitable. But they were achieved by relying on basic grunt work and intelligence, and by harnessing the energy and sense of injustice of workers.

Of course, it's not easy nor always possible to do this, despite the best efforts of unionists and workers. Little could probably have been done to save the textile industry from collapsing in Australia, so powerful were the political and economic forces against it. More recently, inspired by the success of the 2007 'Your Rights at Work' campaign, the ACTU coordinated a series of top-down expensive campaigns to elect federal Labor governments and to change workplace laws. That approach ended in failure — especially the $20 million 'Change the Rules' campaign ahead of the 2019 federal election. The ACTU had wanted legal changes to the Fair Work Act to give unions and workers more rights. No doubt, favourable legal changes would have helped, if implemented, but the strategy was starting from the wrong place.

This is where the closeness of many unions to the Labor Party becomes a weakness, when decisions by unions are too often seen by senior officials through the prism of electoral politics. The reality is that laws have always been stacked against workers in Australia, in favour of business; more pointedly, recent governments have ensured that going on strike is either unlawful or so restricted that it has been near impossible to do. Fresh approaches to empower workers—and to combat inequality—are needed.

According to the law, the RAFFWU is not a registered union, while the UWU has no legal right to represent farm workers in Australia. Under Australia's workplace system, industries are reserved for particular unions. Demarcation disputes occur when unions fight over which union has coverage. Sometimes that can be bitter, even violent, as occurred in 2009 when the AWU and CFMEU fought over which union was entitled to represent construction workers on the West Gate Bridge upgrade. It's a failed system, set up to manage conflict between unions when they represented a far-greater proportion of the workforce. Now much of the workforce is non-unionised. And sometimes when there is a union—such as for fast-food and supermarket workers—the representation it provides is compromised or corrupted. Often, a union has coverage for an industry, but does next to nothing to organise it, or does not have the capacity to do so. The demarcation system should be abolished or ignored.

Farm workers had long gone unorganised, George Robertson told me, as there was a myth that it's 'too hard to organise seasonal workers, and that it's too hard to organise seasonal migrant workers, and that it's too hard to organise seasonal migrant temporary workers. There's that triple challenge, and there's the workers' literal visa status as a barrier. Then there's the period of employment as a barrier.'

He said his experience was that 'this couldn't be further from the truth', that change was possible even among the most exploited workers in the country. 'If you build deep relationships with workers around the principles of unionism, don't take shortcuts, and provide real choices for people about whether they want to step up and take the risk to improve their lives, they'll do it regardless of what the barriers are. It's not about pulling one lever and then, all of a sudden, things become easier, and then that helps the union movement to grow. It's about building the relationships on the ground day to day that will change people's lives.'

Conclusion

This book has been an attempt to describe some of the maladies of wealth and income inequality, wage theft, and precarious work in Australia. It is a dispiriting story of the concentration of power and wealth. I remain hopeful, however, that things can be changed for the better, that we can have a fuller democracy, and that many of us can enjoy better, more equal, lives. For much of the twentieth century, inequality lessened in Australia, and the opportunities of a better life abounded for people from modest backgrounds. This tells us that today's status quo, which is almost the opposite, is not fixed. It can be adapted through a countervailing force, whether organised labour, civil society, or government.

My view is that the former is more important than the latter. A labour movement, along with civil society, when it is strong enough, can change the contours of society, despite a hostile government. It is not the only thing that's needed, but it is vital. It is what Australia experienced through the conservative Menzies years from 1949 to 1966, when inequality fell and was far lower than it is now. This experience coincided with a period of union density considerably higher than it is now. The truth is that pro-worker reforms by a social-democratic government are always vulnerable if there is not a strong labour movement to protect those gains.

At the moment, the prospects for a more equal society appear mixed. In fact, if left to its own devices, the system will keep heading in the other direction. The Albanese government was elected on a relatively modest platform when it came to combating inequality and improving workers' rights. Whatever changes it makes in response to the inevitable crises that all governments face will only endure if there's a robust labour movement to defend them. The demise of the movement—which has gone from representing half the workforce to barely one in ten workers—has allowed neo-liberal capitalism to run rampant. Much of Australia's big-business sector is run in a way to exacerbate that process. The shareholder model, where financial returns are paramount, demands ever-higher profits and returns on capital. That system creates a whirring machine of cost-cutting, wage suppression, and, in the end, widening inequality.

Some of Australia's biggest companies—including Woolworths, the Commonwealth Bank, Coles, and McDonald's—have engaged in wage theft. Barely any sector of corporate Australia has been immune to this approach. The process is sped up further still with private equity, the signature investment method of our neo-liberal age. It takes the logic of profit maximisation to its most extreme levels, handsomely rewarding the private equity firms and their investors. In family-owned or smaller businesses, the logic of this system is sometimes not as strong, creating a more paternalistic, almost familial, model. But this often creates its own problems when under-capitalised and under-developed businesses cut costs and wages, as they cannot compete fairly.

As we've seen, a sense of security at work and elsewhere has vanished for many. Access to secure housing — which, in Australia, is largely gained through ownership — is fast becoming an inherited right for people under forty. Whether it is on the basis of private education, health, or housing, our society is divided between those with access to life-improving opportunities and those without. The emergence of a more heavily class-ridden society means that the dreams of a more equal post-war order are fading. How might this be changed? The most significant force with the potential to do so is organised workers acting collectively.

As part of any rebuilding, there needs to be a public reckoning of how bad things are. Union membership is ageing, while some unions have become complicit in this downward spiral. There needs to be an accounting of the past and a reappraisal of the Accord period: not to condemn the decisions made by union leaders and Labor politicians, but to learn from them. We can now see that enterprise bargaining, privatisation, and economic liberalisation have made life worse for those without marketable skills or an inheritance. Superannuation, won as a workplace gain by unions as a part of the Accord trade-offs, has also morphed into a quasi-tax rort for the rich. Women, typically, are left with a fraction of the retirement savings of men, as the inequality of earnings throughout men and women's working lives follows them into retirement. A generous, publicly funded pension and the heavier taxing of large superannuation balances would be a start at tackling the goal of establishing a fairer society.

There is a need for new, ambitious ideas, which might involve trying and failing at times. Some of the extensive money tied up in property by unions could be liquidated to fund new ideas. With 1.5 million members, even a much-diminished union movement remains the most significant force in civil society. Trade unions are entities with significant historic legacies, and sometimes with giant asset bases. The CFMMEU in Victoria alone, for instance, has assets worth $92 million; the SDA in New South Wales has nearly $70 million worth. Across the movement, there would be property worth billions of dollars. This asset base means that the labour movement can survive, presumably for many decades, even with an ageing, declining membership living on as industrial relics from a previous age. Yet if even a fraction of those assets were liquidated, much could be done. This might include them being used as a seed fund for new ideas and ventures—for example, to bankroll democratically owned and worker-run cooperatives, to rebuild the power of its members, and to transform the society from below. This might sound utopian, but trying new things now is a necessity. Maintaining the status quo will lead to a slow, drawn-out demise.

There are, of course, many things that governments can do to reduce inequality: imposing higher taxes on capital, wealth, and income, and engaging in greater spending on public education, are some of the options open to them. The Albanese Labor government has made few promises in these areas, and over time it should be judged by how it tackles inequality. That will require a willingness to tackle entrenched interests and to explain to a sceptical public the benefits of higher taxation.

The Scandinavian societies are some of the wealthiest and most equal on earth. Their examples show us that working towards a far bigger welfare state with universal access is crucial to reducing inequality.

Another goal is changing the world of work—not being content just to win higher wages. If we want to live in a democracy, work should be democratic, too. Control in most workplaces rests, ultimately, on who has the most capital and therefore the most power. We accept the complete lack of democracy in much of our daily lives as the natural order of things. Instead, decisions should be made by everyone with an interest in an organisation (where it is practical), and not just the owners. As we have seen, Cooperative Power grew from having 200 customers to 2,000 in a few weeks after green-energy company Powershop was bought by Shell, a multinational poster child of environmental degradation. Starting with businesses that require little capital is an ideal way to develop the kind of democratically run society we want to live, work, and participate in. The governance model will need to be developed through trial and error. The modern corporation has developed and been refined over several centuries, so establishing an alternative will need time, too. But, at its core, the new model should be democratic, and not just the token representation of workers and civil society.

Resources should be thrown at organising the most exploited workers. It took seven years and significant resources to change the horticulture sector and to sign up thousands of members. This had previously been regarded as impossible, but the result was significant. The work effort unleashed a new generation of activists — people such as farm worker Mahani Tif, who, when addressing thousands of people, to huge cheers, at a 'Change the Rules' rally, said, 'Farm workers need a better life', 'more respect', better pay, and an 'amnesty'. Her interests as an undocumented worker are little different from those of a university researcher cycling from contract to contract, or a chef working sixty to seventy hours a week, or a fast-food worker unable to take a toilet break. All suffer a deficit of power and of security, and a surfeit of precarity.

None of this will be easy. It is a monumental task to rebuild the power of workers, to create democracy at work, to establish a more equal society, and to change society from below. It cannot be done by a change of government alone. But there is no alternative, unless we want to live in a society of rising precarity, insecurity, and inequality. That would diminish us all.

Acknowledgements

This book would not have been possible without Sarah Toohey, the fiercely intelligent, brave, kind, and amazing person I'm so lucky to spend my life with. She's helped make me a calmer, better person over the last decade and to overcome what, in many ways, was my difficult and tumultuous start to life. Every day I'm inspired by her and the work she has done to expand social housing. It has transformed lives. To my children, Seb, Isaac, and Harriet, you are everything to me. You've put up with the distractions and pressures my work has caused, but still love me and are a source of endless fun, frustration, and everything in between. I love you. I'd also like to acknowledge my mum, Virginia, whose love and support has always been there for me, and also the formidable Carla Hagan, who has been such a significant person in my life. I'm indebted to her.

I'd like to thank Alison Pennington for reading a draft of this book, toughening up the arguments, and for all her intelligent and thoughtful contributions. It has been invaluable. I'd also like to thank Sarah Toohey and my talented friends Adrian Dodd and Jess Kendall for all their important suggestions and edits from reading the draft. All the faults that remain with this work are mine. I'd like to thank my editors at *The Age*, Gay Alcorn and Michael Bachelard, for allowing me to take off time for this project. In particular, I'd like to acknowledge Michael Bachelard, the investigations editor since 2015 (and my direct manager), who has had to endure years of dealing with a stubborn and occasionally annoying reporter. Your encouragement of my work, intelligent editing, and feedback has made me a far better journalist, and the work I've produced that much better.

I'd also like to acknowledge Royce Millar, a terrific investigative journalist and someone whom I've collaborated with — and learnt so much from — on all sorts of projects for the best part of a decade. Much of the work of this book is drawn from my work with Royce over the years. Royce is one of the finest journalists that Victoria has produced, and an incomparably good reporter on corruption, the city, and all sorts of issues that matter. I'd like to thank Henry Rosenbloom for taking the plunge on me to back this, my first book. Scribe and Henry have contributed so much to Melbourne and Australia through backing new writers and publishing books in the public interest.

Finally, this book would not have been possible without the hundreds of workers, unionists, academics, executives, and activists who have spoken to me over the years about wage theft and injustice. I'm indebted to you all for the time you've given me and the trust you've shown in me. Journalism and writing is a collaborative effort, although it is often spoken about as if it is not. This work, whatever its strengths and weaknesses, would be nothing without the help of others.